Congratulations !

Hope you enjoy

faith & trust in the

Love
The Goller's

THE SIMEON
SOLUTION

THE SIMEON SOLUTION

Anne Osborn Poelman

Deseret Book Company
Salt Lake City, Utah

Library of Congress Cataloging-in-Publication Data

Poelman, Anne Osborn, 1943–
    The Simeon Solution : one woman's spiritual odyssey / Anne Osborn Poelman.
      p.   cm.
    ISBN 0-87579-967-1
    1. Poelman, Anne Osborn, 1943– . 2. Mormons—Biography.
3. Mormon Church—Biography. 4. Church of Jesus Christ of Latter-day Saints—Biography. 5. Christian life—Mormon authors.
I. Title.
BX8695.P64A3   1995
289.3'092—dc20
  [B]   94-46883
                                       CIP

Printed in the United States of America

10 9 8 7 6 5 4 3   72082

To those Latter-day Saint men and women
whose lives and steadfast examples
have been a source of great personal inspiration to me.
You know who you are.

Contents

Introduction

As a very young child I wanted to know: Is there a God? If there is, does he truly care about his creation and his children? Does God know me, even if I don't know him? Is he aware of and interested in me as an individual? Does he still work miracles? Would he work them in *my* life?

I don't really think I was unusual. We all want answers to our most deeply felt questions. Each of us is born with an innate longing for our eternal, spiritual home. Life itself is largely an ongoing search for eternal verities.

This book is in part an autobiographical account of my own personal spiritual odyssey. The events related here actually happened. In some instances I have changed the names of certain individuals to preserve their privacy. Writing from the perspective of years or even decades after the dialogues transpired, it is difficult to quote them exactly. I have nevertheless attempted to convey the content and spirit of the interchanges as they took place.

In this book I will share with you how I learned that there is indeed a God, a loving Heavenly Father who is actively and intimately involved in our lives—who knows and cares about us individually and personally.

I will also tell you how I discovered the Lord's church, The

Church of Jesus Christ of Latter-day Saints, and how my faith in its fundamental, straightforward teachings evolved and grew. And finally, I'll share the "Simeon Solution" with you. These simple, gospel-centered principles have given me the confidence to face life's inevitable challenges with equanimity. In the midst of disappointment and uncertainty, we can create our own spiritual "places of safety" that provide a sure haven from the storms of personal adversity.

Please make no mistake about it: This book is written squarely from the center of the Latter-day Saint mainstream. If you are searching for a feminist perspective, look elsewhere. If you hope to find a closet Church rebel, you'll be gravely disappointed.

If what you really want is the perspective of an LDS professional woman who believes that quiet accomplishments speak volumes more than strident polemics, a person who knows that Church members aren't perfect yet is totally committed to the Church, and who trusts implicitly in the eternal perspective, read on. This book is for you.

Chapter 1

The Simeon Solution

It had been one of those golden evenings. You know the kind: seamless. The dinner guests rave enthusiastically about the food, cheerfully help clear the table afterward, then move into the living room where they relax and chat amiably in front of the fireplace. It's snowing outside, adding a snug, cozy feeling to the gathering. Maybe it doesn't snow in your part of the world. Maybe you don't have a fireplace or a living room either. But such friends and such gatherings are universal regardless of the specific setting.

It started innocently enough. The conversation drifted imperceptibly away from comfortable, safe topics toward more controversial ones. In retrospect, it's hard to define precisely when the friendly discussion we had been having edged over the border into outright disagreement. Perhaps it started with a frank but well intentioned question from one of our guests, an accomplished professional woman who was not of our faith. She was curious as to how we Mormon women felt about not holding the priesthood. Did we feel slighted? Unequal? Oppressed?

The questions exposed some of the fissures that exist among women in the Church. No stock, flippant answers such as, "The only priesthood I want to hold is in my arms!" were forthcoming. The responses from the group were candid, deeply felt, and as varied as the women sitting in the room. They covered a broad spectrum that ranged from a historical, contextual perspective to one opinion that Church women ought to press forcefully and publicly for a policy change.

By nature moderate, I seemed to occupy the philosophical middle ground. "Well," I interjected, "I think it's important to look at things from an eternal perspective. One of the things that's very meaningful to me is what I've learned in the temple from the covenants we make there. I think no religion holding as one of its fundamental tenets that the seed of godhood is in every man and every woman and that neither can achieve it without the other could by any reasonable, fair definition be called sexist."

That response precipitated another round of spirited discussion. When the conversation finally subsided a bit and I could express a rejoinder, I decided to try another approach and focused on feelings rather than intellectual argument.

"I'm not sure exactly how to put this. You may think my view is rather simplistic. But to tell you the truth, the whole issue of women and the priesthood really isn't very high on my spiritual 'worry list.' I don't *know* precisely why modern-day women in the Church don't hold priesthood offices. Quite frankly, it doesn't bother me. I'm not even sure it's relevant."

That provoked expressions of surprise. I continued, "I *know* the gospel is true. I also know the restored Church is the Lord's church. And I really believe that if and when it's appropriate, any changes will be made by revelation through the prophet. In the meantime I'm content. I can put issues like women and the priesthood on my spiritual back burner."

One of the men, a well-known and highly respected local physician, had been listening to the interchange quietly. Up to that point he hadn't said a single word. He finally spoke up and added thoughtfully, "Annie, I think I understand and agree with you. What you just said is an example of the Simeon Solution."

"*What* solution?"

"Simeon was the old high priest spoken of briefly in the second chapter of Luke. At the time of the Savior's birth, Judea was occupied by the Romans. The suffering, conquered Jews yearned for the long-promised Messiah, their King of kings, to come and liberate them from the cruel oppressors. Among the Jews living in Jerusalem was Simeon, a just and devout man, who had also patiently waited his entire lifetime to behold the Messiah. He had been told by the Holy Ghost that he would not die before he had seen the Lord's Christ."

He paused a moment, reflecting. "I'm sure Simeon must have had his moments of uncertainty and doubt. But he kept the faith, believing the ancient prophecies and trusting in the revelation of the Holy Ghost. Finally one day Simeon was prompted by the Spirit to go to the temple. While he was there, the Savior's parents arrived bearing the child Jesus. I suppose Joseph and Mary were humble working people who otherwise might have gone unnoticed. But not by Simeon, who instantly recognized Jesus as the promised Messiah.

"The old priest tenderly took the child in his arms. With a heart overflowing with joy and gratitude, he praised God and said, 'Lord, now lettest thou thy servant depart in peace, according to thy word: For mine eyes have seen thy salvation, which thou hast prepared before the face of all people; a light to lighten the Gentiles, and the glory of thy people Israel' (Luke 2:29–32).

"Before that glorious experience in the temple, Simeon had walked by faith alone. After waiting an entire lifetime, at last he *knew* for a certainty that what he had believed and trusted for so many years was true."

The room was completely quiet as we all sat silently pondering his remarks.

He continued: "Faith really does precede the miracle. Faith is the precursor of knowledge. Whenever I encounter a question to which I can find no immediate answer, I adopt Simeon's attitude. I put those issues in the eternal context. I try to wait patiently, in trust and faith. That's what I call the Simeon Solution."

A mental light clicked on and I felt a surge of excitement at the verbalization of a concept I had struggled to express. My friend had put into simple, understandable, and scripturally based terms a process I had been working out for many years through personal experience: the Simeon Solution.

Simeon had indeed kept the faith, waiting most of his life in trusting patience before he beheld the long-awaited Messiah. Simeon was unwavering in his confidence that in due time the ancient prophecies would come to pass and the Lord's personal promise to him would be fulfilled.

Had doubting colleagues challenged the old priest before the momentous event occurred, he might well have answered in the following manner: "No, I haven't seen him—yet. I don't really know why. I don't know all the answers, at least not now, but I believe in the teachings of the prophets with all my heart. I know the scriptures are true."

Whenever I come face-to-face with a contemporary social issue, a practical problem, or even a doctrinal dilemma that bothers me and for which I have no immediate answer, I adopt what our dinner guest so aptly termed the Simeon Solution. Simeon's example gives me the patience and perspective to put unresolved issues temporarily aside. I don't ignore or forget them; I simply move them to a spiritual "back burner." I've learned I don't have to have immediate answers to all my concerns and questions.

With time and experience, I have gradually developed and expanded the concepts my friend and colleague first called the Simeon Solution. Plainly stated, these are:

1. *Trust the Lord.*
2. *Learn to recognize and heed spiritual promptings.*
3. *Focus on the fundamentals.*
4. *Stand firm in the faith.*
5. *Be patient.*
6. *Adopt the eternal perspective.*
7. *Keep the commandments.*
8. *Know the Church is true.*

Sounds simple? It is. It isn't fancy. It isn't sophisticated. It certainly isn't complicated. Some might even say it's *too* basic, but I don't think so. It really works. After all, the concepts are neither new nor revolutionary. In instructing his people, King Benjamin taught that salvation comes to him who puts his trust in the Lord, is diligent in keeping his commandments, and continues in the faith (see Mosiah 4:6).

I believe that every one of us has a real purpose and mission in life. Each of us is truly special, with a unique and important role to fill. The Lord is aware of us. He knows us intimately and individually. He's in charge. He can work miracles, both small and large, in our lives. When we feel anxious, uncertain, or even fearful, our knowledge that the Lord understands, cares, and will guide us—*sometimes in ways we may recognize only in retrospect*—can give us hope, reassurance, and the confidence to cope with adversity.

In this book I will share with you some of my experiences as they illustrate the peace of mind and spirit so aptly expressed by this wonderful concept: the Simeon Solution. I hope it will be as helpful to you as it has been to me.

Chapter 2

A Spiritual Beacon

The big Delta jet, scheduled from Atlanta to Amsterdam, was already more than an hour late. It slowly inched its way up the long line of planes waiting for takeoff clearance from air traffic control. To the west, the wind picked up sharply in advance of a rapidly approaching storm. Just as our long overdue plane finally reached that magic "Number One for Takeoff" designation, the wind suddenly shifted and veered into an entirely new direction.

The plane's intercom crackled to life and the pilot announced with weary resignation, "Sorry, folks, but the control tower has just advised us we need to take off from the opposite end of the runway. So it's going to be a few more minutes."

As if in some elaborately choreographed ballet, the entire conga line of waiting planes wheeled and slowly lumbered down the taxi strip toward the other end of the runway. By the time we were repositioned a towering mass of thunderclouds was boiling furiously over the horizon, racing toward the airport. In a spectacular pyrotechnic display, lightning cracked from the dark underbelly of the clouds and licked the ground hungrily.

The storm struck the airport with short-lived but ferocious intensity. Rain, then hail rattled and bounced along the plane, caroming off the fuselage at crazy angles as the long-suffering

8

passengers cringed inside the stuffy, crowded cabin. An inevitable additional delay ensued while the swiftly moving front passed directly overhead, moved east, and finally blew past the airport toward the distant sea.

The sky, already storm darkened, quickly faded and night fell with the sudden sharpness of a descending guillotine. At last cleared for takeoff, our fully loaded plane slowly accelerated down the runway and lifted off.

After a steep climb and a couple of gradual, lazy circles, we were finally on our way. My husband, Ron, and I were on the initial leg of a round-the-world trip during which I would teach and lecture to medical colleagues while Ron, as a member of the First Quorum of the Seventy, had goodwill meetings with various government officials in India, China, and Southeast Asia. En route at last, we heaved a relieved sigh, leaned our seats back, and settled in for the long overseas flight.

The plane thundered eastward into the foreshortened Atlantic night, occasionally shuddering as powerful gusts from the violent storm raked the fuselage. The seat belt sign remained illuminated most of the time as the captain tried first one altitude, then another, in a vain search for smoother air. Even the cabin crew, navigating the aisles on flight-hardened legs, lurched and staggered as the plane was tossed and buffeted by the unusually heavy winds.

The much delayed dinner, desiccated beyond recognition in the galley's warming ovens, was finally served. The dishes tinkled a monotonous tune as they too danced with the turbulence. We drank only water and ate little, sticking with our long held motto, "Don't waste good calories on bad food."

The meal's remnants were finally cleared and the in-flight movies began. The offerings were banal and uninteresting so we tried to read. Impossible. The plane's nearly constant vibrations in the unsettled air were making us a bit queasy. So we turned out the lights, rolled up in the undersized blankets, squirmed into as comfortable a position as possible, and tried to make the best of a difficult situation.

We dozed fitfully, changing position as aching muscles cried out for periodic relief. The plane finally outran the storm and the engines quieted into a dull, steady drone.

After a seemingly interminable few hours, the bleary-eyed passengers were aroused by another cockpit announcement: "Folks, due to unexpectedly strong tailwinds, we've made up quite a bit of time. We're now only about forty-five minutes behind schedule."

A weak cheer went up from the exhausted passengers. A few people clapped halfheartedly.

The captain continued, "However . . . "

An apprehensive silence settled over the cabin.

"I've got good news and bad news."

Ron and I turned to each other and said simultaneously, "Tell us the bad news first!"

As if in obliging reply, the captain declared, "I'll give you the bad news first. Schipol International Airport in Amsterdam is reporting very dense fog."

Loud groans erupted from irritated passengers who had been taxed beyond the limits of ordinary endurance.

The captain interrupted the chorus of complaints, as if he could hear the expressions of displeasure through the closed cockpit door. "Wait a minute! Now let me tell you the good news. As you know, Schipol is the major air hub for continental Europe. It's often fogged in. But," he added, "it's equipped with the world's most up-to-date electronic instrument-guided landing system. That means planes with advanced avionics such as ours can be landed there in virtually zero-zero conditions: in other words, no ceiling with an 'R.V.R.'—Runway Visibility Range—down to 300 feet or less."

A cautious hope began to dawn.

The captain continued. "This Instrument Landing System, I.L.S. for short, can just about land the plane itself. We lock onto the ground based homing signal and our three onboard autopilot computers pretty much do the rest. So we're going to go right straight in!"

He concluded, "Every other plane will be doing exactly the same thing, timed and spaced perfectly. We've done this hundreds of times. It's actually quite routine. In fact, you probably won't see the ground until we touch down and start taxiing toward the terminal."

Ron raised the window shade. Sure enough. In the thin, gray light of early dawn, all we could see was an impenetrable fog.

"*Ertensoep,*" Ron muttered, recalling long dormant Dutch from his missionary days in the Netherlands.

"What?" I exclaimed.

"Pea soup," he replied. "It's as thick as pea soup."

I smiled a bit nervously. "I've never done this before."

"Well, neither have I. But, fortunately, the pilot has!"

We felt the telltale whine and *thump* as the landing gear was deployed, then sensed a subtle change in engine pitch as the plane descended on its final approach.

It was one of the gentlest landings I've ever experienced. The wheels brushed the runway, then firmly bit into the tarmac as the jet's reverse thrusters roared. The plane braked smoothly and coasted slowly up to the gate. No sweat.

"Good landing," I mumbled to Ron in grateful relief. We

gathered our overcoats and carry-on bags. As we filed toward the hatch door, I spied the captain.

"Nice landing," I repeated.

He was casual, almost nonchalant. "Thanks. But the I.L.S. computers really did it all."

"Could *you* see?"

"Not a thing. Fog was too thick. In fact, you passengers could see before we could. The cockpit's still up in the soup when the rear wheels touch down."

I persisted. "But what about the landing beacon? Don't you have some sort of a screen or something so you can see it?"

"Oh, *that*. Sure," he replied matter-of-factly. "It's a computerized electronic display. Shows our position, proper flight path, and exactly where the center of the runway is. Autopilot flies the plane right down the thing."

Amazing. I shook my head in wonder as we hurried through the jetway in the customary mad dash for Passport Control and Baggage Claim.

Ron and I have discussed that experience many times. It was certainly unnerving to sit in the cramped, confined cabin during that long, stormy flight, then to land when we couldn't even see the ground.

Our apprehension clearly wasn't shared by the captain. *He* could see the beacon that was completely invisible to us. He trusted the accuracy of the I.L.S. system and the reliability of his onboard computers. "Integrity" is the interesting avionics term that means the pilot of an aircraft can be confident the guidance is valid. Though nearly flawless, even the most advanced precision landing systems don't have absolute "integrity." Nevertheless, the strong, ceaseless signals from the electronic beacon on the ground guided our plane more surely than the pilot's own visual sightings could ever have done.

So it is with the influence of the Holy Spirit. Its "integrity" is perfect. It will not fail us if we lock onto its homing beacon. We can indeed land safely, time after time after time.

As I look back on the critical periods in my life, I realize that the most important decisions I've ever made have been guided not by intellect or reason, but by some inner spiritual prompting. Even when I was a child, many years before I joined the Church, it was this way. For lack of a better term I once called that clear but indefinable internal beacon "instinct." I now recognize it for what it was: the promptings of the Holy Spirit. The Lord knew me, even if I didn't really know him.

Trusting implicitly in the light of Christ, using it as a spiritual "navigational aid" to move unafraid and with confidence through life's many foggy moments, is an inestimably precious spiritual gift. Though I didn't know it at the time, to maintain trust in the midst of ambiguity and uncertainty, to "stay the course," is an essential part of the Simeon Solution. It was the first part I learned: to use our spiritual landing beacons even if we can't see the land itself.

For centuries prior to the advent of modern navigational aids such as the I.L.S., the satellite based Global Positioning System, and L.O.R.A.N. (LOng Range Aid to Navigation), simple beacons were used to mark safe deepwater channels as well as denote natural hazards. Lighthouses were built at strategic locations and generations of faithful keepers maintained their lonely vigils so sea-weary sailors could chart their positions.

Many of those old lighthouses still exist today. Although some have been abandoned or transformed into museums, others still serve their time-honored duty. Their beacons sweep ceaselessly, piercing night and fog to guide marine traffic.

The Holy Spirit is likewise a beacon. Its light can penetrate the densest, most perilous fog. Through its promptings we can be warned of life's shoals and reefs, those temptations that would lure us into dangerous waters. The Holy Ghost stands a tireless sentinel to show us the way to personal spiritual safety.

Once we have felt the sure inner beacon of the Holy Ghost and have recognized that still, small voice, we need to relax, trust those spiritual instincts, and rely on the celestial guidance system. It will bring us safely and surely home.

But, you might well ask, what if someone *doesn't* have that particular gift, the gift of inner spiritual certitude?

When we were flying through the dense fog towards Schipol Airport, we certainly couldn't see the I.L.S. beacon that was guiding us toward a soft, safe landing. But the captain could. *He* could see it on the screen, as plain as anything.

Next time I won't worry. I'll trust the pilot. *He* knows, and that's enough for me. In fact, the scriptures clearly tell us that, in the absence of our own personal knowledge and experience, to believe on the words of those who *do* know and see clearly is in itself a spiritual gift (see D&C 46:11–14).

Now let's suppose for a moment that you do have that inner spiritual beacon. You have felt the strength of its powerful signal. It has guided and comforted you on more than one occasion. What if all of a sudden, right in the middle of some horrifically important, highly critical time in your life, just at the time you need it most, *it shuts off!* Blank screen. No signal.

You pray in desperation, pleading for guidance. Nothing. Cosmic silence. What do you do? Panic? Abandon your prayers in disillusionment? Of course not. First of all, the signal itself—that is, the prompting of the Holy Ghost—never shuts off although our own spiritual receptors, our personal "electronic display screens," may at times become temporarily disconnected.

What should we do? If our spiritual receptors are dysfunctional because of unresolved transgression, the answer is obvious and the pathway to repentance clearly marked. However, the question becomes even more poignant when we're living the gospel as best we can, keeping the commandments, and faithfully serving the Lord. If the heavens are strangely silent and our righteous prayers seem to go unanswered, what then?

What would that airline captain have done if the I.L.S. system had suddenly, inexplicably shut down when the plane was on final approach? Crash in the fog? Fortunately, that's highly unlikely.

I recently asked an experienced pilot what might happen in such a circumstance. "Well," he replied, "The routine procedure would be to abort the landing and perform what we call a 'go-around.' We put the plane in a steep emergency climb and circle around for another attempt."

That makes sense. Give it some time, circle around once or twice to get your bearings, and then try again.

"Are there other options?" I persisted. "Like maybe take the last known instrument readings and compute the landing approach from that?"

He grinned. "That's not exactly the recommended first choice! Everything's happening so fast. But we do have what we call the 'scoreboard,' which shows the last available information. You could probably do it from that if you absolutely had to."

That backup scenario is also intriguing: The pilot quickly takes the last clear reading from the system before it shut down, extrapolates the coordinates from there, and stays the course.

One of life's universal, most important mortal experiences is learning to live by faith and "fly in the fog." As a new convert to the Church, I was deeply moved by the account of Lehi's dream in the Book of Mormon (see 1 Nephi 8:1–33). I imagined myself as one of the "numberless concourses of people" who were pressing forward, striving valiantly first to find, then stay on the path that led to the tree of life. I could almost feel their growing alarm and ensuing despair as an "exceedingly great mist of darkness" arose and completely enveloped them.

Some became confused and were overcome by the dense, vaporous darkness. Many stumbled and wandered off the narrow path, losing their way. I hoped I wouldn't be one of that unfortunate group.

Others, surrounded by the same seemingly impenetrable fog, caught hold of an iron rod that ran along the path. Using the rod as a guide, they continued to press their way forward through the darkness "even until they did come forth and partake of the fruit of the tree."

However, some who had tasted the fruit then became distracted by the scornful scoffing of onlookers. Ashamed, they turned away and they too became lost. I winced and fervently hoped I wouldn't be one of that group either.

The final group, also blinded by the dark mists but clinging to the rod that guided the way, pressed forward to reach the tree. Refusing to become distracted, and ignoring the taunts of others, they fell down in gratitude as they reached their objective and thankfully partook of the fruit. I vowed I'd try to become part of that faithful group.

There surely will be times in each of our lives when we can't see the pathway, when everything around us feels confused and uncertain. We will indeed be surrounded by our own personal "mists of darkness." During those challenging, unsettling times, it is essential to navigate by faith, relying on the guidance of the Holy Ghost. If in times of crisis you can't sense the celestial homing beacon, *recall the last time you felt that inspiration and, using that experience as a spiritual "marker buoy," extrapolate your course from there.*

Once you've set your own course, ask the Lord for reassurance that you're headed in the right direction. The peace, serenity, and quiet confidence that washes over us when we're on the right "flight path" is in itself an answer to heartfelt prayer.

The Lord sometimes leaves us to struggle a bit, learning to work out the answers to our dilemmas ourselves. "But, behold, I say unto you, that you must study it out in your mind; *then* you must ask me if it be right" (D&C 9:8; italics added).

Finally, personal revelation is not constant. As Elder Dallin H. Oaks has said, "We believe in *continuing* revelation, not *continuous* revelation. We are often left to work out problems, without the dictation or specific direction of the Spirit. That is part of the experience we must have in mortality" (*Teaching by the Spirit*, 1994 New Mission Presidents' Seminar).

I suspect that Simeon's revelation that he would actually behold the Savior may have come to him only once. Then he apparently spent a lifetime in trust, believing and staying the course extrapolated from the glorious but long-ago experience. Following Simeon's simple but effective example can bring peace and fulfillment into our lives.

Chapter 3

Roots

For better or worse, our adult selves often strongly reflect our origins and childhood experiences. My own roots are in Culver, Indiana, one of the thousands of small towns that dot the rural American landscape.

Growing up was a sometimes delightful, often painful process that in my case was accentuated by our small community's social hierarchy. Our town was then—and remains to this day—a study in stark contrasts. It is rescued from Midwestern ordinariness by a beautiful nearby lake and a renowned private secondary school, Culver Military Academy.

Since the early 1900s, Lake Maxinkuckee has been a favorite summer vacation spot for monied families and wealthy suburbanites from Chicago, Detroit, Fort Wayne, and Indianapolis. Many of those families had for generations sent their sons (and, much more recently, their daughters) to the Academy.

Socially, Culver was divided into five distinct entities. At the pinnacle were the elite, "old money" Lake families. Next, clinging a bit precariously to the social apex firmly occupied by those blue-blooded families, were the "new rich." These were big-city lawyers, stockbrokers, medical specialists, and investment bankers whose own skills and productivity had earned them the rewards and social perquisites of a Lakeside weekend retreat. They built large, ostentatious new homes next to the rambling, slightly tatty but respectably chic "cottages" of the Old Families.

Next on the social totem were the Academy faculty, a number of whom had Ph.D. or master's degrees from Ivy League schools. Salaries were low but the prestige accorded faculty members made up for their relatively penurious circumstances.

Below the Academy faculty were the native townspeople, unimaginatively nicknamed "Townies." Most were hardworking, ordinary folks who provided essential services to the Academy and Lake populace: stuff like plumbing, laundry and dry cleaning, and secretarial services. Others were small businessmen, proprietors of struggling enterprises with hopeful names such as "The Don Trone Shoppe" and "Quality Grocers."

At the very bottom of Culver society were the farmers. Hardy, fiercely independent folk with sunburned, weathered faces, they lived outside the town at addresses like R.R. (for "Rural Route") #2 and County Road 17. Their habitual dress, faded and worn denim overalls called "Can't Bust 'Ems" (for the logo embossed on their copper buttons), would decades later be considered quite chic. But in those days they were decidedly unfashionable—especially as they often smelled faintly of the morning's chores!

I was a Townie. Translated, that meant the next-to-bottom rung of the social ladder. Fitting this all together reminds me of a cartoon I once saw of two congressmen standing outside the Capitol Building in Washington. One is saying to the other, "No, I'm not a member of the In Group. But the Out Group has an In Group, and I'm a member of that!"

In fact, I wasn't even in the In Group of the Out Group (i.e., the Townies). Growing up, I was definitely a tomboy. I climbed trees and played basketball with the boys. I was also *big*. Nearly five feet ten inches tall by the time I reached junior high school, I was usually the biggest kid in my class. Not the biggest girl—the biggest kid!

I was plain. And worst of all, I was smart. That was the real social kiss of death. I was always chosen first for athletic games but was dead last on the unwritten but immutable date-bait rankings. Sure, I was named "Most Likely to Succeed" in the yearbook. True, my academic achievements were occasionally written up in the town's tiny weekly newspaper, the *Culver Citizen*. But I was never mentioned in the school's social columns.

All of us are, to a greater or lesser degree, haunted by memories of failure. I'm sometimes asked, "Did you ever fail at *anything*?" The answer is a definite yes. When I flat-out flunked a course in biostatistics during medical school, I was left with some rueful embarassment but no residual psychic scars. By contrast, the result of a hopeful but misguided attempt at social success remains vividly etched in my memory.

As a child I wanted absolutely more than anything in the world to be a cheerleader. I yearned for the automatic prestige and virtually guaranteed social acceptance that accompanied membership in that elite group. So in tenth grade I decided to try out for the junior varsity ("jayvee") squad. There were only sixteen girls in our entire class. Eight were trying out for the jayvee squad; four would make it.

The cheerleader selection committee was composed of two teachers and all the boys on the jayvee basketball team. Confident of their own status (almost by definition, "athlete" seemed to mean "cool"), the boys expressed their superiority in the kind of mocking teenage cruelty that reached its zenith during the annual cheerleader tryouts.

The hopeful girls first lined up for physical inspection as the initial groupings were customarily made according to height and appearance. I was at least four inches taller than the next-biggest girl. Strike one.

Mixing and matching candidates, the committee next asked various combinations to lead practice cheers. The jayvee basketball team formed a makeshift "pep club." They were supposed to chant loudly as the girls pranced around on the gym floor. When my turn finally came, they didn't yell. They didn't chant. They snickered. I do have to admit that I didn't have the requisite crispness and smartness to my movements. I was undeniably enthusiastic but a bit awkward. Strike two.

I later learned that some of the girls always fudged the rules by practicing together prior to tryouts so they would look especially sharp. I hadn't been invited to those private rehearsals. Strike three.

One by one, the Chosen were motioned out of the lineup. As they shrieked with joy, the rest of us stood forlornly in the background and then silently filed out of the gymnasium. As I passed, one of the team members (who I had secretly always wished would ask me for a date but who of course never did) looked directly at me and scornfully laughed out loud.

I was humiliated. I felt ugly, inadequate, and undesirable. More than thirty years later, that memory is still incredibly vivid. The whole cheerleading experience severely damaged my self-esteem and left feelings that I would struggle with for years. It inflicted a wound that would heal only with the help of the gospel perspective.

A few years ago I saw the same basketball player at a high school reunion. His athletic physique and teenage good looks had eroded considerably with age. I'm ashamed to admit it, but I felt a rush of secret satisfaction! I was only fifteen when I made my failed try for the cheerleading squad; my girlish humiliation was, I think, understandable. But my uncharitable reaction as a grown woman was truly immature. I hadn't yet learned the patience and forbearance and their by-product of forgiveness that are part of the Simeon Solution.

During a more recent visit to my hometown, I decided to stroll by the old school. The building itself had been demolished years before. Several school districts, including our own Union Township, had been consolidated into a spanking new, modern campus constructed on the edge of town. Only the old gymnasium remained, now in use as part of the elementary school complex.

It was early summer and school was out. Surprised at my sudden diffidence, I timidly tried the gym door. It clicked open. I stepped inside and thirty-five years instantaneously vanished. I stood there overwhelmed by a flood of memories.

The silence was deafening. Sunlight filtered through the high, opaque windows. Dust motes twinkled, then hung motionless, suspended in the flat, stale air.

At first I could scarcely believe it was the same place. I remembered it as a huge, cavernous auditorium. It wasn't.

It's so small! I thought, astonished.

Then, *It seems so insignificant.*

Why did something so minor seem like such a big deal? I asked myself.

The answer came from deep inside my soul. *Then* I hadn't known who I really was. I sought approval and validation from external sources. *Now,* thirty-five years later, I do indeed know who I am, what I believe, what I stand for.

Who am I? A Latter-day Saint woman with a deep, abiding testimony of the gospel. I'm a wife, the eternal companion of my beloved husband and best friend. I'm a doctor and a healer. All three roles complement and enhance each other.

What do I believe? It's really quite simple and straightforward:

1. Jesus is the Christ, the son of God, the Savior and the Redeemer of the whole world.
2. Joseph Smith was indeed a prophet of God.
3. The Book of Mormon is the word of God.
4. The Church is true.
5. The President of the Church is a prophet, seer, and revelator.

Those principles form the bedrock foundation of my belief. They are sufficient. To be sure, our religion involves more complex concepts and doctrinal subtleties. But by focusing on the fundamentals I have become—and remain—firmly rooted and grounded in the faith. Moreover, I feel comfortable and confident in that faith.

Do I know all the answers to all my questions? Certainly not! But that really doesn't concern me. I refuse to be distracted by peripheral issues and the doctrinal sidebars that some would use to weaken our testimonies of the gospel. To those I apply the Simeon Solution: I have full trust that if and when the answers come, they will be in perfect harmony with what I already know. And what I know is, quite simply, that the gospel is true. There is great peace and serenity in that very simplicity.

So, with those basic concepts firmly embedded in my soul, I made one last pilgrimage on that return visit to my old hometown.

A couple of years before those traumatic cheerleader tryouts, I had borrowed my brother's pocketknife and climbed a towering, smooth-barked Indiana sycamore. There, in a secret childhood ritual never shared with anyone else, I had carved a heart with my initials and the basketball player's.

I found that old tree once more. I hesitated, then with some misgivings climbed its dizzying heights and searched. Yes. The roughly carved heart was there, faint but still visible. And I realized with a surge of gratitude that though the scar in the tree remained, the wounds in my own heart and psyche had healed.

Chapter 4

Ugly Duckling

Recently several of my women colleagues and I were discussing the painful rites and rituals of teenage passage. I ruefully recounted the cheerleading episode, noting how only time, distance, and religious perspective had helped heal the wounds inflicted by that experience.

Mary, a strikingly handsome woman now in her early forties, waited until I concluded and then flatly stated, "When I was growing up I was ugly too."

We all chimed in, "No, you weren't ugly. You just *thought* you were ugly!"

"No," she corrected, "I really *was* ugly."

"Did you wear glasses?" another colleague asked, as if that explained everything.

"Yes. They were thick, pointy ones that turned up on the sides and had rhinestone frames. I had mousey brown hair. And on top of everything else I wore braces on my teeth and had pimples!"

"Don't you feel attractive now? You really are beautiful," I observed as the others nodded emphatic agreement.

"No. And I don't think I ever will."

Another woman present in that gathering is a brilliant

physician and highly successful businesswoman. She always dresses superbly and has a sparkling personality.

"Peggy," I mused, "*you* look like what I wanted to be when I was growing up. You know: You're blonde. You're petite. You're cute. When we had our 'fifties party several years ago you could still fit into your poodle skirt!"

"It wasn't like what you think at all," she replied. "The boys called me Frigid Fritsche. It was awful."

We were astonished. "Why?"

Peggy grew serious. "If you're blonde, petite, and cute, the boys assume you're good for only one thing."

We all nodded knowingly.

"And when you don't 'put out,'" she continued, "you're not good for anything. They taunted me."

That was a revelation to me. How could being cute possibly be a burden? Indeed it can be, and a heavy one at that. Hard to believe though it is, perhaps being pretty while you're growing up is in some ways even more difficult than being plain. The unspoken assumption seems to be that anyone who is truly attractive can't really have brains—that would be *too* unfair, wouldn't it!

My younger sister, Lucy, was cute too. She had dates—lots of them. Miracle of miracles, she even dated Academy boys! *She* was a cheerleader. *She* was a frequent item in the school paper gossip columns. *She* was popular. I envied her.

Lucy has told me she was halfway through medical school before she really realized she also had brains. As a child she felt strongly reinforced by friends and family for being cute, not smart. I didn't know how she really felt until many years later.

As adults Lucy and I have become very close friends and colleagues as well as sisters. One evening we were talking about self-image and growing up. In a burst of candor I exclaimed,

"Lucy, when we were growing up you made me feel ugly, *ugly*, UGLY!"

She replied heatedly, "Annie, when we were growing up you made me feel stupid, *stupid*, STUPID!"

I stared at her dumbfounded. For a moment neither of us said a word. Then we both burst into tears and hugged each other.

"Lucy, you're definitely not stupid!"

"Annie, you're really beautiful!"

My sister and I helped each other realize we really were okay. Lucy is now a nationally recognized professor of pediatrics, has been named to a number of high-level government advisory councils and committees, presently serves as associate vice president for health sciences at the University of Utah, and has been nominated for the presidency of a major university in the Midwest.

Lucy, dumb? Hardly! Yet despite her notable professional successes, I suspect somewhere deep inside her still dwells the teenage girl who felt valued for beauty and whose brains were largely unrecognized. I do know that for many years way down inside me was the insecure, plain, small-town girl who felt like an ugly duckling.

Such feelings seem, in varying degrees, to be almost universal. We may not all feel physically unattractive; some may feel dumb, inadequate, or just plain ordinary. Others, burdened by guilt or unresolved transgression, may feel spiritually disfigured.

Perhaps you or one of your children was the only one not invited to a popular classmate's birthday party. Perhaps you were always the last one chosen in playground games. Or maybe you overheard a whispered comment that undermined your self-image. Seemingly secure people often suffer feelings of inadequacy and unacceptability—even cheerleaders and athletes!

Men often feel that way, too. My husband, Ron, by anyone's

standards a handsome, distinguished-looking man (I admit I'm prejudiced, but I have lots of independent verification of this), grew up in a family so poor they didn't live on the "wrong side" of the railroad tracks, they literally lived in between two sets of tracks!

Ron's father, Hendrik, the son of working-class immigrants, had to leave home in order to attend high school. Hendrik's father regarded education beyond the legally mandated eighth grade as an unnecessary indulgence. Hendrik finished high school but college was a dream beyond hope.

Despite his humble origins, Hendrik Poelman served many years as a bishop and in a stake presidency. His gentle and loving nature, innate spirituality, and gift of discernment blessed the lives of countless Latter-day Saints. I never knew Henry Poelman; he died many years before Ron and I were married. I'm sure I would have liked him. Because he was so accepting of others, I think he would have liked me too.

When Ron was still in grade school, Hendrik Poelman moved his young family into a one bedroom home in central Salt Lake City. It was barely inside the boundaries of the East High School district, an area that encompassed the comfortable, upper middle class neighborhoods surrounding the University of Utah. Most East High graduates went on to college; many received advanced degrees.

Although he couldn't afford to send his own children to the University, Hendrik Poelman cherished the ideal of higher education. He wanted his family to associate with people who valued education and self-improvement.

The Poelman home was a humble one. The parents and baby occupied the sole bedroom; the three older boys slept on a screened-in porch. As Ron puts it, "In the summertime it was adventuresome; in the winter it was character building!" By modern standards, the family income was well below the poverty line. No time or money was available for athletics or after-school activities.

Ron went to work at age ten selling magazine subscriptions. By age twelve he had a paper route. At fourteen he got a job at the old Dunford Bakery. Mondays through Fridays, Ron arose at three A.M., worked for four hours, then returned home and dressed for school. After school he worked at paper routes and a variety of miscellaneous jobs. Ron recalls pushing his bicycle heavily laden with magazines up the long hill past East High, his eyes lowered in hopes that the football players and cheerleaders wouldn't notice him.

Ron was tall and darkly handsome. Trust me; I've seen his high school yearbooks! He was an honor student, bright and hungry for knowledge. But he never felt popular. He was self-conscious, acutely aware of his serviceable but decidedly unfashionable hand-me-down clothes.

Hmmmm. Ronald Poelman, ugly duckling?

Before our marriage, I was the University's faculty adviser to Mortar Board, the national honorary society for student leaders (read: Big Women on Campus). When I told the girls Ron and I were engaged, they were excited for me and enthralled with our whirlwind romance. Several of them exclaimed, "My mother went to school with Elder Poelman and has talked about him for *years*! She thought he was a real dreamboat. But he never ever asked her out."

I told Ron. He was completely surprised. "*Me?*" he exclaimed. "Why didn't they ever tell me!"

Case in point: The handsomest of all the General Authorities (at least to me) clearly felt like an ugly duckling.

I then asked him, "How do you feel now, after all these years?"

"It's hard to describe. In some respects I still don't feel particularly attractive. But in others, I feel like the fairy-tale ugly duckling that grew up into a swan."

"Why?"

He answered simply, "Because you love me. And because I know my Brethren do too."

Ugly duckling images may persist long past childhood, their subliminal whispers still a potent influence on adult self-image. We may never completely rid ourselves of the insecurities generated by those ancient feelings, but we can put aside old hurts and limit their detrimental effects on our current behavior.

How can we mute the ability of such powerful memories to wound anew? One way is by placing them in eternal perspective. In retrospect, my failure to make the jayvee cheerleading squad seems almost laughably insignificant and my emotional reaction amazingly immature. The Adult Annie says, with a mental shrug, "No big deal, really."

The Teenage Annie protests, "But at the time, it seemed like a monumental catastrophe!"

The operative word here is *seemed*. In his introduction to *The Story of Philosophy*, historian Will Durant wrote: "So much of our lives is meaningless, a self-cancelling vacillation and futility; we strive with the chaos about us and within; but we would believe all the while that there is something vital and significant in us, could we but decipher our own souls. We want to understand. . . . We want to seize the value and perspective of passing things, and so to pull ourselves up out of the maelstrom of daily circumstance. *We want to know that the little things are little, and the big things big, before it is too late; we want to see things now as they will seem forever—'in the light of eternity'"* (Garden City, New York: Garden City Publishing, 1943, p. 1; italics added).

How can we know which things are inconsequential and which are truly important? The prophet Jacob answered that question succinctly: "The Spirit speaketh the truth and lieth not. Wherefore, *it speaketh of things as they really are, and of things as they really will be*; wherefore, these things are manifested unto us plainly, for the salvation of our souls" (Jacob 4:13; italics added).

If we are spiritually sensitive, we can know that the little things are indeed little and the big things are big. Part of the Simeon Solution is learning to put our experiences and choices into eternal perspective. Childhood memories, although not erased, no longer loom so large.

The converse is also true. Many dilemmas that perplex and discourage us today may, with the wisdom of perspective, seem comparatively insignificant tomorrow. Today's concerns often evaporate when viewed with hard-won future maturity.

One way to overcome negative experiences (from childhood or adulthood) is to seek surroundings and circumstances that encourage and uplift rather than undermine and destroy. For example, I always feel terrific after I've taught our ward's Gospel Doctrine class. I work hard to make the lessons both informative and inspiring; in turn the class members, most of whom are older and more experienced than I am, express their appreciation and enthusiasm for my efforts and their affection for me personally.

Another great, healing step is to love and serve others. If we strive to enhance the self-image of others rather than focus intently on our own inward esteem, we will surely find a spiritual "balm of Gilead."

As we lift and encourage others, we ourselves are also lifted. As we seek to build others through selfless service, we in turn are built. "Wherefore, he that preacheth and he that receiveth, understand one another, and both are edified and rejoice together" (D&C 50:22). As we edify each other, our souls soar in mutual rejoicing.

When suffering personally, if we notice the suffering of others and succor them, we in turn are succored by the Savior.

Even the Savior, the Creator and Redeemer of the world, likely experienced "ugly duckling" feelings. After all, the scriptures tell us that he had "no beauty that we should desire him" (Isaiah 53:2) and that he would actually experience the feeling of our own human infirmities: "For we have not an high priest which cannot be touched with the feeling of our infirmities; but was in all points tempted like as we are, yet without sin" (Hebrews 4:15). And "He will take upon him their infirmities, that his bowels may be filled with mercy, according to the flesh, that he may know according to the flesh how to succor his people according to their infirmities" (Alma 7:12).

He who was despised, mocked, and rejected of men overcame the bonds of death and rose triumphant to become Lord of lords and King of kings, the Savior and Redeemer of the World, our teacher, exemplar, and friend. Whenever we feel lonely, discouraged, or even depressed, there is surely One who understands.

The Savior himself knows what we know, has experienced what we experience, and indeed feels what we feel. Knowing that fact can comfort us and give us hope, enabling us to put aside old hurts and look to the future with confidence. Confident and assured in the Savior's love, we can remain focused, rooted, and grounded in the gospel fundamentals. If we focus on the fundamentals and keep the Lord's commandments, we will be prepared to hear and heed the promptings of the Spirit as the Lord guides and directs us. Then miracles can happen in our lives.

Chapter 5

Belonging

In the popular musical *West Side Story,* ill-fated lovers make plans to escape from their conflict-filled environment to a place of peace and safety. The poignant song they sing, "There's a Place for Us," expresses the deep yearning we all feel to find a place where we can truly be accepted, where we really belong.

After the cheerleading debacle, the door I had hoped would open into the wonderful world of social acceptance was summarily slammed shut. Once the initial humiliation wore off a bit, I decided to focus on my strengths instead of wistfully wishing for attributes (namely cuteness and popularity) that I didn't possess. I redoubled my efforts in one arena where I knew I might truly excel: using intelligence.

It wasn't easy. As was true of many rural towns, the Culver public schools combined kindergarten through twelfth grade. Our tiny high school was housed in an antiquated building with woefully inadequate facilities. Tax revenues were low and budgets were tight.

In those days all the children of similar age were in the same class. There were no advanced placement courses and each class plodded along at a snail-like pace, only as fast as the slowest student could manage.

Mom and Dad augmented our uneven education with frequent trips to Chicago and its wonderful public museums, designed summer reading projects for us, and helped me build a rudimentary laboratory in our family's single bathroom. The core of my laboratory was an old chemistry set purchased from a mail-order catalog and some discarded glassware scavenged from high school science classes. It was spartan but I was very proud of it.

The little bathroom laboratory hummed with activity. I built a crude Wilson cloud chamber to look for subatomic ("cosmic") particles, but my real love was the biological sciences.

It was a wonderful time to be a science nut. The late 1950s and early 1960s have accurately been called the golden age of biochemistry. Watson and Crick deciphered the structure of deoxyribonucleic acid, the double helix molecule that holds the entire human genetic code in a space far smaller than the head of a pin. "DNA" became a household word as discoveries tumbled forth from laboratories in Boston, Bethesda, and Cambridge, England. I was entranced by the majesty, mystery, and elegant simplicity of the fabulous molecule.

Time magazine and more serious, semiprofessional publications like *Scientific American* ran feature articles on the human body and its intricately choreographed Mardi Gras of cells. Eager to learn everything I could, I devoured every available magazine and scoured the local public library for more. After I quickly exhausted more conventional sources, I discovered a course catalogue from Purdue University. It was a couple of years out of date but sure enough, a course on nucleic acids was listed under the biochemistry department! Too innocent to know from its triple digit course number that it was a graduate seminar meant for Ph.D. students only and that unsolicited inquiries are sometimes ignored, I wrote to the professor who taught the course. I told him of my interest in the subject, explained the limited resources available to a small-town high school student, and asked for more information than could be found in the magazines available in local libraries.

To my delight—and the professor's credit—he responded to the letter by sending me a substantial packet of reading materials. A warm correspondence ensued and he invited me to visit his campus laboratory. I was thrilled!

There was only one minor problem. The university was eighty miles away. I was only sixteen years old and had just received my driver's license. To this day I still can't believe my parents actually did it, but they let me skip school and drive the family station wagon to Purdue's main campus in West Lafayette, Indiana. Perhaps they knew instinctively how important this opportunity was to me.

I hardly slept the night before the trip and woke long before dawn. My father gave me directions (which turned out to be reasonably good but not perfect, resulting in an unplanned detour or two) and, in case I stayed late, arranged an overnight room for me in the Student Union.

Professor Axelrod was waiting when I arrived. He welcomed me enthusiastically and spent the entire day showing me around the Life Sciences complex. He treated me like visiting royalty! As we relaxed in his office at the end of that long but exhilarating day, I felt bold enough to ask him a pointed question. "Dr. Axelrod," I said, "you've just spent an entire day with me. You don't even teach undergraduates, only advanced graduate students. Why would you spend so much time with a high school student who knows very little about biochemistry?"

He grew quiet and contemplative, leaning back in his chair with a faraway expression. A smile flickered across his face at some distant memory.

I waited.

"Well, Anne," he finally replied, "I guess it's because I feel an individual can only discover science once. We experience the thrill of that discovery just once. The only way anyone can ever recapture those feelings is by helping someone else, like an Anne Osborn, find the same thing."

I've never forgotten his words. How true! And it doesn't matter *what* that shared experience is. It can be something as simple as teaching a child to swim or ride a bicycle without training wheels. Or it can be as profound and eternally significant as sharing the gospel with someone who hears the marvelous message of the restored Church for the very first time.

I spent the next summer on the Purdue University campus as one of eighty high school students in a program sponsored by the National Science Foundation designed to interest young people in scientific research. Forty of us were at Purdue studying biological sciences; another forty were at Massachusetts Institute of Technology studying physical sciences and mathematics.

It was tough. Everyone was bright, competitive, and extremely hardworking. We spent the mornings in classes taught by full professors who were experts in their fields. In the afternoons each student worked in a laboratory doing a basic research project. I did experiments in Dr. Axelrod's laboratory. Three evenings a week we had seminars. The rest of the time—what there was of it—we had free for study and social activities.

To my astonishment, I actually was one of the more popular girls. Imagine that! I had dates galore. I discovered you don't have to be a cheerleader to be socially successful. Just find a group of people who share your goals, interests, and, most importantly, strong, positive values. Among my fellow NSF students brains were admired, not scorned. Good grades were a mark of achievement. Achievement was valued, not denigrated.

The summer science school was one of the watershed events in my life. For perhaps the very first time I felt good about who I was, appreciated and accepted for the real me. I also began to have an inkling—just a glimpse, mind you, not yet a really strong sense—of how I might use the gifts I *did* have (not the ones I wished for but didn't possess) to serve others.

We all need to learn who we are and where we belong. But that personal revelation may dawn gradually, evolving over many years and through varied experiences.

I have asked Ron when he first felt that he was no longer an outsider, that he truly *belonged*. His answer was immediate and simple: "On my mission."

"Why then?"

"Because the other elders had the same goals and values I did. To learn. To serve. To be faithful. Those things weren't regarded as goody-goody, they were just simply *good*."

I understood. After all these years, those missionaries still get together. They really enjoy each other's company. I've met many of them and they are as disparate a group as I can imagine. Some are city folks. Others come from rural areas. Their occupations vary from skilled manual labor to academic and professional pursuits. They cover the whole political spectrum. But three things bind them undeniably together: their love for each other, their knowledge that the gospel is true, and their shared commitment to the Church.

Although it is undeniably painful to feel like an outsider, an "ugly duckling," the glorious joy of belonging can lift you far beyond that pain. If you haven't found the comfort and satisfaction of acceptance, be patient. There are people like you out there somewhere—especially in the Church.

Chapter 6

The Quest Begins

Small rural towns are filled with churches. Culver, my hometown, had at least a dozen different varieties: Methodist, Lutheran, Evangelical United Brethren, Episcopalian (very "high church," theologically neutral, and thus appropriate for the Academy students and faculty), and, of course, Roman Catholic.

The Osborns were all staunch Methodists. My mother chaired the building committee for the new church, a lovely Williamsburg colonial-style structure. My father was the lay leader. They were steadfast, loyal pillars of the church.

I loved the Culver Methodist church. It was homey, warm, and comfortably, predictably familiar. Yet I somehow sensed something was missing, although I wasn't sure what it was. I don't know whether Mom and Dad knew then how I felt. I suspect maybe they did but we didn't discuss it.

In the long-standing Protestant tradition, ministers came and went every four or five years or so. Some were wonderful, truly Christlike men. Others weren't particularly exemplary. One, a troubled and angry man who openly and publicly doubted the divinity of Jesus Christ, eventually left the ministry to become a clinical psychologist.

Church attendance—and therefore the church's financial

fortunes—waxed and waned according to the minister's popularity. Faithful members (like my parents) attended regardless of who occupied the pulpit. Others, disliking the sermons or personal style of a particular minister, would leave in a huff and refuse to attend meetings or contribute until a new pastor arrived.

My brother, sister, and I went to Sunday School each week. Religion both fascinated and unsettled me. Filled with some vague, indefinable longing as well as intense curiosity about all beliefs, I read every book on religion in the town library. I peppered our minister and the Sunday School teachers with incessant, pointed questions. Most of the time they couldn't answer them; they were usually at a loss to explain what I thought were fundamental inconsistencies in the accepted dogma.

To my parents' distress, I eventually struck up a friendship with the local Catholic priest. We spent long hours discussing and arguing theology. Had Mom or Dad asked, I could have told them the major reason was because Father Lenk was the best educated and most knowledgeable of all the local clergy. But he didn't have the answers I sought either.

When I finally left our small town for far-off California to attend Stanford University, I was determined to continue my odyssey, my search for some as yet undefined personal Holy Grail. I visited a number of churches and briefly joined the popular First Methodist Church of Palo Alto.

I became increasingly dissatisfied with the thin theological soup served up each Sunday in the local churches. As was true of many liberal mainstream Protestant denominations in the 'sixties, the "God is dead" (or if not dead, at least irrelevant) refrain drowned out songs of faith while the major pulpit messages seemed to center around the popular cause of the week. One week it was the Vietnam War. Another time it was environmental concerns. On still other occasions some social cause occupied center stage. Although I very much enjoyed the personal associations with other members, I eventually gave up and stopped going to church altogether.

During the remainder of my undergraduate days at Stanford and my Ph.D. program at Harvard, I attended church only when I returned to Culver, largely out of courtesy to my parents and the desire to see our longtime friends and neighbors.

Except for the famed Tabernacle Choir I had heard little about the Mormons. The Church of Jesus Christ of Latter-day Saints received only a little space in one of my favorite childhood references, *Life* magazine's book on *The World's Great Religions*. Brigham Young, the "Great Colonizer," was briefly mentioned in our high school history text. Joseph Smith's name never even appeared.

I had visited lots of different churches but certainly had no intention of ever visiting the Mormon church. My sole encounter with the Mormons had been during a cross-country automobile trip when my sister and I stopped overnight in Salt Lake City on our way to California. During a hurried, self-guided tour of Temple Square just prior to its evening closing, I had formed two distinctly amusing but quite erroneous impressions of the Mormons: They revered golden seagulls and worshipped somebody named Joseph Smith!

I do remember one odd thing about that brief first encounter with the Mormons. A large crowd had gathered in the Assembly Hall on Temple Square for some sort of meeting. It was a balmy autumn evening so my sister and I stood outside the door and peeked in. One by one a number of young people—even younger than we were—stood confident and unafraid in front of the congregation. With obvious emotion, each spoke of his feelings about his faith. The word *testimony* was mentioned frequently, something like, "I know the Church is true." Lots about Jesus Christ.

I felt vaguely disturbed. *Something* was definitely happening there. I didn't know what it was and it bothered me.

Despite the earnestness of the speakers, there seemed to be a certain repetitiveness in what they were saying. After a while we left. In the press of beginning the autumn quarter at Stanford, I soon forgot about the experience.

Senior year was filled with coursework, a time-consuming honors research project, and application to graduate schools. Religion became the farthest thing from my mind. In the era of the Berkeley free speech movement and the nascent Vietnam War protests, religion was decidedly unfashionable anyway. Liberation theology was the only socially acceptable theology in the student lexicon.

After graduating from Stanford I spent a year in the psychology Ph.D. program at Harvard University. My doctoral research project was at Massachusetts General Hospital. One day in late autumn I was crossing from the Charles Street subway station toward the hospital. It suddenly struck me, as clearly as if I'd heard it spoken aloud, that I was in the wrong place doing the wrong thing.

I was so startled at the thought that I stopped abruptly and stood immobilized. The thought came to me: I should go to medical school. And at only one place—back at Stanford.

I had no idea what was happening. How could I know, with such absolute, undeniable certainty, that it was the right thing to do? It wasn't rational. It wasn't logical. It just felt *right*.

I'd never even considered medical school. I regarded the Stanford premeds as a bunch of ego-driven, hypercompetitive, narrowly focused prima donnas. Me? One of *them*?

I first called my parents. I didn't know much about medical school except that it was long, hard, and very expensive. I knew I would lose my graduate school fellowships and would need financial support from the family.

Once my parents recovered from their initial shock at the surprise announcement, Dad gulped and said quietly, "Well, Annie. That's quite a change. But we're behind you one hundred percent. I've always told you we would provide as much education as you wanted and needed."

Bless him. He trusted me. And I trusted my instincts.

Although I didn't recognize it until many years later, what I had experienced and called "instinct" was really the prompting of the Spirit. The Lord was aware of me even if I wasn't aware of him.

I telephoned my senior thesis adviser at Stanford and told him of my proposed change in career plans. He was surprised but said he'd see what he could do. For starters, he promised to speak with the Dean of Admissions in the medical school.

The adviser returned my call the next day. "I spoke with the Dean and he looked at your academic transcript. You haven't taken all the prerequisites."

"No," I admitted.

"You haven't taken the MCAT (Medical College Admissions Test) either."

"No, but I did pretty well on the Graduate Record Exam," I answered hopefully.

He harrumphed, "Doesn't count," and continued. "You haven't even filled out an application."

"I'll send one in right away."

"Too late. The deadline was six weeks ago." He paused, then

43

asked, "Just *why* do you think you want to do this? It seems like a very abrupt decision."

I felt desperate. How could I possibly explain? "I—well, you might not believe . . ." I stammered.

"Never mind," he replied. "I was just upset that you'd give up working toward a Harvard Ph.D. The Dean said it was highly unusual but, on the basis of your undergraduate record, they'll admit you anyway. Just get the prerequisites finished by the time you show up here in September."

I whooped with excitement. "All right!"

I could feel his grin over two thousand miles of telephone wire. "Oh, and by the way," he added, "you need to take the MCAT. Just for the record. Won't matter anyway but we don't want the Dean to look foolish if anyone ever asks!"

A bit dazed by the abrupt change in direction, I added chemistry to my already full load of graduate courses, went to Boston University night school for physics, and took a full year of organic chemistry in a concentrated, eight-week summer course. I finished just in time to drive to California and register for the fall quarter of medical school.

At the time, I didn't recognize that whole episode for what it was: the Lord working a genuine miracle in my life. It was, especially in retrospect, an astonishing experience. Now having been on a medical school faculty for twenty years, I know things like that simply don't happen. But it did. How? It certainly wasn't my own doing. I have only one satisfactory explanation: The Lord guides and prompts us, sometimes without our even recognizing his influence for what it truly is. *If it's right, the Lord will open the way.*

Our Heavenly Father does indeed take an active interest in his children's lives. The Creator of a million million galaxies and worlds without number is aware of each one of us. The Savior told his disciples that the very hairs of their heads were all numbered (see Matthew 10:30). Imagine that! The Lord is intimately involved in the details, not just the general scheme of things.

The concept that the God of the universe can and does make us individual objects of divine attention, even intervention, is staggering but true. The Lord didn't set the galaxies in motion and then retire to some remote corner of the universe to observe his handiwork.

I didn't know it at the time, but the first simple principle of the Simeon Solution clicked subconsciously into place:

1. Trust the Lord.

The Lord is in charge. He knows us and our needs far better than we do. If we will just put our trust and confidence in him, Heavenly Father can work in our lives to make extraordinary things happen.

Chapter 7

Meet the Mormons

The first two years of medical school passed in a blur. We were immersed in biochemistry, physiology, gross anatomy, and other required classes with little time for anything other than our demanding studies. Sundays were prized as "catch up on sleep" days. Nobody that I knew ever went to church.

My long dormant interest in religion was eventually revived when I discovered, quite by accident, that one of the best and most beloved professors in the medical school was a Latter-day Saint. This man, highly respected in his field, won the students' affection with his devotion to teaching and to his family, as well as with the exemplary way he conducted his life.

I'd never personally met a real live Mormon before. I was curious. And puzzled. An internationally acclaimed scientist who worshipped seagulls and somebody named Joseph Smith? It just didn't fit. I was too embarrassed to ask how he managed to accommodate such apparently incompatible beliefs.

I eventually forgot about the whole thing.

During the brief summer break prior to beginning the third year's grueling rotations through surgery, pediatrics, internal medicine, and other clinical specialties, I volunteered to teach water safety instructor classes for the American Red Cross. The Red

46

Cross National Aquatics School was an intensive, two-week course held annually at a YMCA camp in the high Sierra mountains. Between two and three hundred college-age students from throughout the country gathered there as soon as school was out to obtain Water Safety Instructor and First Aid certification before going to their summer jobs.

The faculty was a heterogeneous group. Some were professional Red Cross staffers; others, many of them coaches and physical education teachers, were volunteers. Most had been doing this for years. There were a few "greenies." I was most definitely among the latter.

One of the experienced hands was an older man from southern California who impressed me with his gentle demeanor and quiet dignity. The lucky students who were in his First Aid classes adored him.

Early June was unusually hot and dry that year. One day during the lunch break, another faculty member got up to get refills on drinks and was taking requests. He looked at the older man and grinned mischievously. "Well, Max!" he said. "How's about I get you a glass of nice cold iced tea?"

Max smiled. "Thanks for the offer. You know I don't drink coffee or tea. But I'd sure like another glass of milk!"

I was surprised. I guessed Max was in his mid-sixties. What was a man his age doing drinking a quart of milk each meal? Distinctly abnormal, I thought.

One of the other faculty members leaned across the table and whispered loudly, "Oh, don't mind old Max. He doesn't drink tea because he's one of those crazy Mormons!"

Crazy? Somehow I didn't think so. Different? Definitely. He didn't smoke; he didn't drink alcohol, coffee, or tea. But the only two Mormons I knew, Max and the medical school professor, were exemplary men. However odd their beliefs might have seemed, their faith evidently made a tremendous difference in the way they lived and interacted with others.

After lunch I drew him aside. "Max," I said, "I understand you're a Mormon."

"That's right," he answered.

"Well," I continued, "I don't know anything about the Mormon religion. In fact, I only know one other Mormon—one of our professors at the medical school belongs to your church. I admire both of you very much. I want to know what makes the difference in your lives."

"It's our faith," he replied quietly.

"I thought that might be the case. Would you mind telling me something about your church and how it's different from other churches?"

Unlike most other Mormons I've known since then, he didn't immediately launch into a discussion about the Church. "Why do you want to know?" he asked cautiously.

I was a bit taken aback. I hadn't anticipated such a question. "I'm not really sure," I confessed. "I grew up in the Methodist church. I liked it but always felt something was missing. I've visited a bunch of other churches but they all seem the same. I feel like I'm being preached at, prayed at, sung at. I finally gave up looking."

Max must have decided that my interest was sincere and that my intent was not to poke fun at or ridicule his beliefs. So every night after supper the two of us sat out on the porch of the main lodge. While everyone else played volleyball or tossed horseshoes, we discussed religion.

He told me about angels, buried gold plates from a long vanished civilization, and a boy-prophet named Joseph Smith. I don't mind telling you, it seemed really strange. Unbelievable. But what kept piquing my interest was the deep, undeniable effect their religion seemed to have on the only two Mormons I had ever known. That—and their sincerity—I couldn't deny.

The two-week camp passed swiftly. Before I knew it, it was time to leave. As I was packing my gear, Max came to say goodbye. I could tell by his expression that something more was on his mind.

He came to the point quickly. "Anne, when you get back to Palo Alto and Stanford, you ought to look up the local Mormon church and try it out."

It would have been impolite to express my profound skepticism, so I kept silent.

Max grew serious. "Go," he said firmly, then looked me straight in the eye. "I've never been to Palo Alto. Don't know anything about it. But I'm going to make you two promises. The first is this: If you visit the Mormon church you'll find the most wonderful group of people you've ever met. In fact, you'll feel like you've known them all your life."

I listened intently as he continued.

"And the second is: if you go, *and go with an open mind*," he emphasized, "you'll find a faith with depth and meaning and joy greater than anything you ever believed was possible."

Wow. Those were two really big-time promises.

During the long drive from the Sierras back to Palo Alto, I couldn't get Max's promises out of my mind. That last conversation bothered me, as he had evidently intended. It even scared me just a little.

In retrospect, I think I know why I felt that small, icy trickle of fear. On the one hand, if I did go and the Mormon church was just like all the others, I'd be disappointed once again. On the other— and I think this really was the scariest part—if what Max had said *was* true and the Mormon church was indeed all he'd promised it would be, I would have some major, life-changing decisions to make.

The whole dilemma made me feel profoundly uneasy. The combination of hope and curiosity finally got the best of me, and I decided I would try it out. The easiest way would be to call the professor at his office and ask if I could go to church on Sunday with his family. No luck. His secretary told me they were gone for the summer and wouldn't be back in town until September.

Somehow I just couldn't wait three months. So I pulled out the Palo Alto telephone directory.

Found the Yellow Pages.

Looked up "Churches."

No "Mormon Church."

An unexpected rush of disappointment. Then I remembered that the correct name was The Church of Jesus Christ of Latter-day Saints.

Turned the page back.

And groaned inwardly. Now I found more than I'd bargained for. There were *lots* of "Mormon" churches listed. Two in Palo Alto. Two at Stanford. Another in nearby Menlo Park. A couple more in Redwood City. How was I supposed to choose?

I finally decided the logical thing was to pick one where I knew the streets and could at least find the place. Menlo Park. There were two numbers listed; heart inexplicably pounding, I called the first one. No answer.

Sigh of relief. "Lord," I thought silently, "you know at least I tried!"

But I didn't feel good about letting it go. So I tried the second number (which I now know was the bishop's home phone).

A childish voice said, "Hello?"

"Is your daddy home?" I inquired.

"No."

"Is your mommy home?"

"No."

I was getting desperate. "Well," I continued, "how about a big brother or sister?"

"No. They're outside playing."

Giving up, I finally got more specific. "I need some information about the Mormon church."

"Well," the small voice answered slowly, "we don't drink coffee or tea . . . "

I almost had to pick myself off the floor, I laughed so hard. "I *know* you all don't drink that stuff," I was finally able to reply. "What I really want to know is what time you and your family go to church on Sunday morning."

"Well," the voice said, "my daddy goes at six o'clock!"

I almost hung up right then and there.

The voice continued. "My big brother goes at nine."

"What about you and your mother and your big sister?"

"Oh!" the voice replied confidently. "We go at ten-thirty!"

That was more like it. I decided that was when I probably ought to show up.

Sunday dawned bright and clear, a truly gorgeous summer day. I almost chickened out, using the easy appeal of a long walk or bicycle ride as a handy excuse. But the more I thought about *not* going, the worse I felt.

"Oh, what the heck?" I finally thought. "The worst that could happen is I could waste a nice Sunday morning." Bathed and dressed, I headed for the Menlo Park "ward," timing my arrival just prior to 10:30 A.M.

Max had given me rather specific instructions for such an occasion. "When you go the first time," he'd said (and I guess he knew I would), "you ask to see a man they call the 'bishop.' Tell him you're not a Mormon but want to know something about the Church."

That made me suspicious. I was dead certain I would be surrounded by eager Mormons, salivating at the prospect of a fresh convert. So I decided I'd fool them. I wouldn't say anything to anybody. I'd sneak in the back and spy on them—see how they behaved when they didn't know someone was watching!

I parked and went into the building at precisely 10:30. I was astonished. *No one* was in the chapel. *Everyone* was in the foyer, talking, laughing, and hugging. Kids were running around with handfuls of Cheerios. I'd have put the background noise level at about forty decibels at least. It was chaotic, but it was a warm, friendly, even inviting kind of disorder.

Sticking to my original plan, I said nothing to anyone and slipped into the back of the chapel so I could sit on the last row and observe the proceedings.

More surprises. There was no altar. No cross, either. No collection plates. No candles. No dignified minister in clerical collar and black robe. A couple of men in business suits, a nicely dressed young woman, and a child occupied the elevated pews that faced the congregation.

The service (which I later discovered was the Sunday School opening exercises) began unceremoniously with some informal announcements and a hymn (thankfully it was one by Charles Wesley; being an old Methodist, I knew it by heart). Then the child gave a scripture reading and the young woman followed with a brief but excellent talk. Everyone sang another hymn, this time written by someone named Pratt. It was totally unfamiliar but inexplicably moving.

Finally young men conducted something I recognized as similar to communion: the sacrament. Uncertain whether it was appropriate to participate, I passed it up, feeling a wistful pang.

As I sat there alone, observing the amateur-led worship service, I felt strangely touched. A tear came to my eye and burned its hot furrow down my cheek. Filled with conflicting feelings and embarrassed at this unexpected rush of raw emotion, I was seized by an intense desire to escape. *Get out of there!*

I stood up suddenly and ran out the back door to the parking lot, intending never to return to that strangely evocative place.

And stopped.

A voice inside my mind said, as clearly and distinctly as if it were an auditory experience, "Anne, turn around and go back!"

I did. In that moment my life changed instantaneously and would never again be the same. Ever.

I look back on that experience as *the* central event, the defining moment of my life, the fulcrum on which everything else subsequently rests. Had I ignored that still small voice or convinced myself it was the product of an overactive imagination, the things I now hold most precious and dear in my life might never have happened.

So, even unrecognized and unarticulated at the time, another principle of what would eventually become the Simeon Solution was added to the first:

2. Learn to recognize and heed promptings from the Lord.

Listen to and heed promptings from the Holy Ghost! If we're open to those spiritual impressions, the Lord will guide our lives. We can trust him. He will open the right doors, at the right time, and in the right sequence.

Chapter 8

Investigator

I must have been quite a sight, walking back into that church half blinded by unaccustomed tears. Oddly enough, no one seemed to notice. I would soon learn that Mormons cry a lot (and unashamedly so) when they express deeply felt emotions.

I stopped the first person I saw. "Excuse me," I croaked. "Can you tell me where the, uh, 'Inquirers Class' is?"

I had the wrong name but he certainly knew what I needed. "Why, sure!" he replied warmly. "In fact, I'll take you there myself!"

The Menlo Park Ward had a very active investigators' program. A number of members and their guests had already gathered in the crowded room. The class was led by an enthusiastic teacher, a man who had previously served as the ward's bishop.

One of the class members had brought clippings from the religion section of the local newspaper. They were part of a recent weekly series reporting on how teenagers felt about their churches. He first read an article written by some young people from my own church. It was a broad, rather stinging indictment of organized religion's failures in general and their own congregation's shortcomings in particular.

I felt a bit defensive but kept quiet.

He next read from an article written by teenagers from the Menlo Park Ward. The contrast was striking, even compelling. These young people obviously felt quite different about their own religious experiences. They were actually looking forward to taking two prime years of their lives (at their own expense, no less) to serve as missionaries for their church.

A lively discussion ensued, centered around how the Mormon church was similar to—and different from—other churches. I didn't participate in the discussion but listened intently. After class was over, I went up to ask the teacher about a few theological loose ends I thought had been left untied.

He launched into an elaborate explanation, then suddenly stopped right in the middle of a sentence. "Is this your first visit to a Mormon church?" he asked.

I nodded.

"Why did you come? You came alone, sat by yourself, and didn't seem to know anyone."

Thinking he was gracious not to notice my streaked mascara and tearstained face, I told him about Max's promises and the personal example the Stanford professor had set.

"Yes," he agreed, "he and his family are terrific people. They're members of the Palo Alto First Ward."

I wondered aloud if Mormons somehow all knew each other.

He laughed. "Almost. In fact, when you came in everyone noticed and wondered who you were."

So much for anonymity. I paused a moment, then somehow felt compelled to tell this man about what had happened when I had attempted to leave the chapel, intending never to return again.

More tears, this time both mine and his. Neither of us felt the least bit embarrassed. "Look," he finally said, "we can't stand here and talk about that very special spiritual experience and discuss all your questions about Mormon theology in ten minutes after Sunday School. Why don't you come to our home for dinner tonight? Meet my family. If you want to hear more, we'll tell you. And if you don't," he smiled, "come and have a good meal with us anyway."

I accepted and tucked his quickly drawn map with their address and telephone number into my purse. "By the way," I said without even thinking, "I have a really nice dog, Tish. She's a golden retriever. She's very well behaved and loves children. Could I bring her, too?"

Without a moment's hesitation he replied, "Of course. The kids would be delighted. She'd probably enjoy a swim in our pool!"

At the appointed time, Tish and I appeared on their doorstep. To this day I'm not sure which one of us they were most excited to see, but we were both welcomed warmly.

During dinner the children surreptitiously slipped Tish tidbits under the table, giggling as her delicate licks tickled their hands. After the dinner dishes were cleared and put away, we adjourned to the living room for dessert and more serious discussion. I thought the children would leave but they joined us, clearly intent on participating. With a grunt of contentment, Tish curled up near 'Becca, the next-to-youngest child, who thoughtfully patted and scratched her in all her favorite itchy spots.

The whole family promptly launched into an enthusiastic discussion about what they called "the Church." Bishop Hunt took the lead, but was frequently interrupted as each child interjected enthusiastic comments and personal observations.

After a couple of hours of this friendly but nonstop give-and-take discussion, I was exhausted. The kids were still going strong!

Mercifully, Bishop Hunt finally stopped the conversation. "You know," he said, "we've talked a lot tonight about the Church. But it's been in a somewhat random, hit-or-miss fashion. I don't know if you'd be interested or not, but we have some people in our church who, uh—well, being a doctor or at least *almost* a doctor, I think you'd understand—more or less specialize in teaching people such as yourself."

I *was* interested.

"It comes in six easy lessons," he grinned. "If you'd like to hear them, we can arrange to have the teaching done right here in our own home." We set a date for later that week.

The "teaching specialists" turned out to be two very competent, highly educated stake missionaries. I believe one of them had two doctorates; the other had only one, but he also had two master's degrees. From the onset I somehow regarded the discussions more as a debating match than a lesson. Although we all clearly enjoyed the lively interchanges, from the missionaries' point of view we weren't making much "progress." In a tactical change, one evening Bishop Hunt informed me they had decided to call in what they termed the "full-time elders."

"Aha!" I thought triumphantly. "*Now* we're going to get somewhere. Finally I'm going to hear the *real* authorities. At last, the definitive stuff!"

To my utter astonishment, the "elders" turned out to be two young men, clearly even younger than I was. To the family's evident dismay, in the interval between their invitation and the appointed evening one of their favorite "elders" had been replaced by a brand-new, totally unfamiliar one.

I now know that the innocent "greenie" elder (preferably straight off the farm in Idaho or southern Utah) who successfully teaches a stubborn investigator after better educated, more sophisticated missionaries have been stymied is a storied Mormon cliché.

But it sometimes really happens. This particular green elder had been in the Palo Alto district less than a week and it was now his turn to give the very first discussion of his mission. To me.

Following the introductions, I watched in amazement as the eager but nervous young man set up a flannel board his mother had used to teach children in Sunday School. He had a bunch of cutout paper figures that he stuck on the board as he spoke haltingly.

"Sister Osborn," he began, "we came to Earth as spirit children of our Father in Heaven." He put an earthlike globe on the board.

"Sister Osborn," he continued, "when we came here in mortality, a 'veil' was placed between us and heaven." He then stuck some cotton on the board that looked like clouds. Sort of.

Every two or three sentences he'd have a memory lapse and forget what he was supposed to say. When he hit those uncertain moments, he would fill in the awkward gap by repeatedly saying, "Sister Osborn, I *know* the gospel is true."

That kind of flat, all-encompassing statement made me fume. Like others I've known since then, I said somewhat heatedly, "Elder, I don't see how anyone can *know* intangible things like that are 'true.' Why don't you just say 'I *believe* the gospel is true'? That seems more accurate anyway."

He paused and gulped. "Well, Sister Osborn," he finally said as he looked me straight in the eye, "I guess I just believe it so hard I know it's true!"

How can anyone argue with such an earnest, deeply felt testimony? I really couldn't. The sincere, simple expression of that young elder's uncomplicated but deep faith touched me in a way that all the high-powered intellectual arguments and discussions with the stake missionaries had failed to do. But it still wasn't enough. I wanted to know for myself. I *had* to know on my own.

The elders asked me to pray with them. I felt uncomfortable about doing it and it didn't seem to help a great deal. They suggested I read the Book of Mormon and highlighted some particularly pertinent scriptures for me. Because I was more comfortable with the New Testament, they also read to me from the book of James: "If any of you lack wisdom, let him ask of God . . . and it shall be given him." Then the big *but:* "But let him ask in faith, nothing wavering" (James 1:5–6).

I felt I did lack wisdom, particularly the spiritual kind. But could I really ask in faith? I shook my head. Faith was something I was striving to develop, not something I already possessed. Then I remembered Paul's definition: "Now faith is the substance of things hoped for, the evidence of things not seen" (Hebrews 11:1).

In dawning hope I asked God to let me know if the Mormon church was true.

I'm not sure what kind of response I expected. The ghostly finger of God mysteriously writing on a wall? A visitation? A light? An angel appearing? That would have done quite nicely, thank you. Even a repeat of that inner voice I had felt that first Sunday at church would have been convincing.

There was nothing. Not even a whisper.

Then the elders read Alma 32:26–28 to me. Although I didn't accept the Book of Mormon as "scripture," these particular verses were hauntingly beautiful:

"Now, as I said concerning faith—that it was not a perfect knowledge—even *so it is with my words. Ye cannot know of their surety at first, unto perfection, any more than faith is a perfect knowledge.*

"But behold, if ye will *awake and arouse your faculties,* even to an *experiment upon my words,* and *exercise a particle of faith, yea, even if ye can no more than desire to believe, let this desire work in you,* even until ye believe in a manner that ye can *give place for a portion of my words.*

"Now, we will compare the word unto a seed. Now, if ye give place, that a seed may be planted in your heart, behold, if it be a true seed, or a good seed, if ye do not cast it out by your unbelief, that ye will resist the Spirit of the Lord, behold, it will begin to swell within your breasts; and when you feel these swelling motions, *ye will begin to say within yourselves—It must needs be that this is a good seed, or that the word is good, for it beginneth to enlarge my soul; yea, it beginneth to enlighten my understanding, yea, it beginneth to be delicious to me"* (Alma 32:26–28; italics added).

Those moving verses certainly described my situation. I resonated to the concept that if you can't actually believe, you can at least start with the *desire* to believe and let that desire gradually work and grow within you. At that point all I really had was an inexplicable, instinctive feeling that I was on the track of something infinitely worthwhile and supremely important.

Instinct is one thing. Faith is another. And knowledge is an entirely different story. I yearned to *know.* That desire was at least a beginning, however modest. Alma said it should count for something. I was positive I would get results from my earnest, repeated petitions to the Lord.

Still nothing.

The elders carefully reread Alma's sermon to me, pointing out that the desire to believe was only the first step. The next stage required work, real spiritual "heavy lifting." Well, why not? I accepted the scientific method, so the concept of actually "experimenting" with Alma's words appealed to me. Instead of resisting the Spirit by focusing on doctrinal doubts and uncertainty, I decided to follow Alma's simple, straightforward counsel to make a small place for a portion of his teachings. Let them work. Then examine and judge the results.

Bit by bit, I gradually realized that the things I was being taught were familiar. It seemed as though I had somehow always known them. They were enlightening my understanding and expanding my soul. They felt good—yes, even delicious.

But it wasn't enough. Although I didn't need to have a perfect knowledge, I did need some kind of confirmation that my instincts were correct, that I wasn't deceiving myself, that I was indeed on the right track.

One evening the elders turned to chapter nine of the Doctrine and Covenants, in which the Lord admonishes Oliver Cowdery first to "study it out in your mind" and *then* ask God if it is right. That made sense. Do the homework, put in your spiritual "sweat equity," as it were. Instead of asking the Lord to do it all, take responsibility for the decision. Make up your own mind. If your conclusion is correct, the Lord will answer by making you feel good about it. If it's the wrong course of action, the scripture said you would feel confused and experience a "stupor of thought."

I liked that concept a lot. Instead of nagging the Lord for an answer, you could and should seek it within yourself. Then ask for confirmation and validation of your decision.

I studied. I pondered. I prayed that the Lord would bless my efforts and find them an acceptable offering. Then on a balmy summer evening when I at last felt ready, I hiked into the foothills above the University.

Alone in the silence, I knelt down and prayed aloud. "Father," I pleaded, "I've worked hard. I've studied. I really do believe the gospel is true. I feel the Mormon church is truly your church. I've decided to go ahead and join. If I'm right and this is the correct decision, please, oh please, let me feel good about it. Let me *know*.

And if it's not, *please* tell me before I make a terrible mistake. I ask this in the name of thy Beloved Son, Jesus Christ."

As soon as I concluded, I knew I had my answer. I didn't see anything. I didn't hear the voice either. What I *did* feel was an incredible peace of mind. A calm confidence washed over me and I knew without doubt I had made the right choice: to become a Mormon.

Chapter 9

No More Strangers

The baptismal date was set. As the designated day drew closer, I felt unexpected yet understandable discomfort. This was going to be a major change in my life. Was it really the right thing to do? Increasingly uncertain and anxious, I wondered if this were the Lord's way of warning me about an impending mistake. Not so, the alarmed elders said as they tried unsuccessfully to reassure me. They explained it was merely Satan's influence, a last-ditch attempt to dissuade me from selecting the right path.

Attributing such doubts to a malignant adversary, whatever the name, was an easy, convenient explanation for the elders. It was singularly unhelpful for me. "The Devil made me do it!" was a hackneyed line from tired old comedy routines that I'd never found particularly amusing. In a holdover from my liberal Protestant days, I wasn't convinced such a being even existed. I'd been taught that evil was merely the absence of good and that only the ignorant or unsophisticated believed that satanic beings were actual entities.

My commitment wavered as the good feelings that had once felt so strong evaporated like water on a hot summer sidewalk. I was sorely tempted to call the whole thing off. Uncertainty seemed to feed on itself as I began to worry about all the things I didn't know about the Mormons and their beliefs. First one question, then another arose as nagging doubts sprouted and grew like weeds in an abandoned garden.

It really didn't seem fair. After all, I had made my decision once, hadn't I? And felt it was right. That should have been sufficient. I hadn't expected to be assailed by second thoughts. My prayers for help seemed to go unanswered as I felt I had been left very much alone to struggle with indecision and doubt.

Longing for reassurance, I once again turned to the scriptures. I reread Alma 32, this time focusing on the later verses. There was no question in my mind that I *had* felt peace and inner rejoicing as the desire to believe worked deep within my soul. As I had nurtured that embryonic faith by study and prayer, it had indeed sprouted, grown, and begun to bear fruit. I *did* feel that the word was a good seed, that it was even beginning "to be delicious unto me." Then that wonderful feeling seemed to vanish into thin air. What had happened?

Almost by accident—or so it seemed—I stumbled across Alma's earlier words to the recalcitrant Nephites. When he asked those who had once experienced a change of heart, "If ye have felt to sing the song of redeeming love, . . . can ye feel so now?" (Alma 5:26) it seemed as though the revered prophet were speaking directly to me across the chasm of millennia. I realized I had indeed experienced a profound change of heart. I recalled what that joyous, wonderful "song of the heart" had once felt like.

The more I thought about it, the more I realized that finding the Church and the gospel wasn't really a discovery after all. It wasn't new. Quite the opposite: It was more like recognizing something I'd actually known for a very long time, maybe even eternities.

It was true that I didn't know everything, nor did I have the answers to all my questions neatly delineated. But the fundamental pieces were all in place and they were consistent. I realized I did have a firm, undeniable testimony that God lives and that Jesus is the Christ. I knew that Joseph Smith was indeed a prophet of God, that the Book of Mormon is the word of God, and that the Church is true. For heaven's sake, what more did I truly need?

The clear, calm confidence I had felt when I initially decided to join the Church returned. Two weeks after the young elders began teaching me the missionary discussions, I was baptized.

Baptisms are exhilarating, joyous events. To my surprise, this very special occasion was literally as well as figuratively regarded by my new ward friends as a birthday celebration. There were even very nice gifts: personalized scriptures, a pocket hymnal, and a number of books that formed the nucleus of my growing Church library. Even Tish was remembered with a gaily wrapped box of her favorite dog biscuits!

I half expected that after all the whoop-de-do was over and another convert was checked off on some imaginary missionary score sheet, things would return to normal and I would be left to fit in as best I could. Not so. That ward truly followed Moroni's admonition: "And after they had been received unto baptism, and were wrought upon and cleansed by the power of the Holy Ghost, they were numbered among the people of the church of Christ; *and their names were taken, that they might be remembered and nourished by the good word of God, to keep them in the right way,* to keep them continually watchful unto prayer, *relying alone upon the merits of Christ, who was the author and the finisher of their faith.*

"And the church did meet together oft, to fast and to pray, and to speak one with another concerning the welfare of their souls.

"And they did meet together oft to partake of bread and wine, in remembrance of the Lord Jesus" (Moroni 6:4–6; italics added).

In the weeks after my baptism, I received follow-up doctrinal discussions with the missionaries and attentive personal visits from my new "home teachers" and "visiting teachers." Frequent invitations to family dinners and ward social activities helped make me feel an integral part of the Church. I was asked to speak in sacrament services and other meetings throughout the stake.

A few days after I was baptized, I received a call from the ward clerk. The bishop wanted to see me. Too new in the Church to know that such requests usually elicit curiosity, perhaps even a twinge of anxiety, I showed up at the appointed time.

After greeting me warmly and inviting me to sit down, the bishop came straight to the point. "Sister Osborn," he said with a smile, "after prayerful consideration, the bishopric is calling you to teach the Sunday School class for sixteen year olds."

I was completely taken aback. "I'd be happy to do whatever I'm asked," I replied, surprised. "But I really don't know all that much about the Church as yet. How can I teach what I don't know?"

"You love the Lord. You know the basic principles. I think you'll be a wonderfully enthusiastic teacher. That's sufficient. Besides which," he grinned, "this is a real lively group of kids. They ask lots of questions. You can all study and learn together!"

And so we did. We were a classic example of the scriptural admonition, "Wherefore, he that preacheth and he that receiveth, understand one another, and both are edified and rejoice together" (D&C 50:22).

As I reflect on those weeks and months after my baptism, I realize what a critical, even vulnerable time that is for a new convert. It is important to become integrated into the ward family.

Prompt calls to serve in an appropriate capacity surely help. The spiritual seeds that have been so successfully planted must also be carefully tended and nurtured by both the new member and the local congregation. As the winds of adversity blow—and they surely do—even the most spiritually fertile topsoil can be swept away by a storm of opposition. Left untended, those tender young plantings of spiritual rebirth will struggle and may even wither from neglect.

I was fortunate. I was not only numbered among the Saints, I was also nurtured, encouraged, and accepted.

I felt wonderful. I *belonged*. Max was right; I really did feel as though I'd known these people all my life. I was, to paraphrase Paul, no more a stranger but a fellow-citizen of the household of God (see Ephesians 2:19).

Perhaps inevitably, the postbaptismal period was not without its challenges. There were lots of "ups." Some hurdles. And a few "downs" (more about those later). The only thing that made me really uneasy was the potential reaction of friends and colleagues. Most of all, I worried about my family. We were very close and I loved them very much. Would they understand? I decided to wait until I was home on vacation to tell them about my newfound faith, hoping the good effect I felt the Church was having in my life would be readily apparent.

It wasn't, at least not initially. They were all understandably concerned at this sudden, completely unexpected development. Although my brother and sister-in-law joined the Church soon after I did, acceptance and approval from other family members evolved more gradually as they observed the positive effects of the gospel in my life.

A foretaste of possible adverse reactions from colleagues and friends came within a week of the baptism. One morning I found a pink message slip in my mailbox at the medical school. An ominous sign. The only other time I had received one was when I had flunked the biostatistics course.

I swallowed hard. The message was from my faculty adviser. "See me ASAP," it read. Nothing else.

I spent an anxious morning before I could break away from my duties for lunch. I half ran, half walked to his office and knocked, almost hoping he would be away. He wasn't.

"Come in!" his gruff voiced boomed. "You have a minute?"

I nodded.

"Well then, sit down. We need to talk."

I sat.

He paused a moment, frowning. "How are you doing?" he said. "I haven't seen you much this summer."

"I've been really busy, what with studying for the National Board Exams and then with clerkships starting."

"Yes, yes, I know," he said impatiently. "What I really mean is, are you okay? Is everything all right?"

I gave a silent, inward sigh of relief. It wasn't about some performance deficiency after all. "Yes, I'm just fine. Really."

He pressed. "You're not in any trouble?"

I was puzzled. "No, of course not."

"Did somebody, uh, your boyfriend, you know—jilt you or something?"

What a strange question. I appreciated his obvious concern but it really wasn't any of his business. "No. I'm not even dating anyone steadily now."

He paused, making up his mind, then forged ahead. "I heard a rumor about you."

I still didn't get it. "What kind of rumor?" I asked warily.

"Well," he answered uncomfortably, "that you'd sort of gone off the deep end."

"Well, I haven't!" I replied somewhat testily. "I don't have a clue what you're talking about."

He got specific. "I heard you went and joined some kind of religious cult."

Now I got it. "I joined the Mormon church, if that's what you mean. And they're *not* a cult," I emphasized.

He was clearly unconvinced. "Why would you do such a thing?" he persisted.

Perhaps it was foolish to respond the way I did. But I was so excited and enthusiastic about my newfound faith that I couldn't help myself. Naively expecting him to share my joy, I briefly told him about my experience with the Church, concluding with hearing that inner voice.

He pounced. "Aha!" he exclaimed almost triumphantly. "A voice, you say!"

"Well, not an actual, audible voice or anything like that," I said hastily. "It was more like a still, small 'something.' You know, an impression. Like a whisper. Something I *felt* deep inside myself. You know what I mean?" I finally concluded hopefully, thus ignoring the First Law of Holes. (When you're in one, quit digging!)

He clearly did *not* know. His face grew stern and challenging. "How do you know that it wasn't just yourself talking to yourself?"

Good question. A very good question indeed. "I just sort of *know*," I answered lamely, at a loss to explain.

"Humph," he snorted somewhat derisively, but he let it drop.

The interview over, I thanked him for his interest and concern, then beat a quick retreat.

I've thought about that interchange many times as I have pondered the issue he raised. How can we be guided spiritually? How do we *know*? The answer involves several simple but interrelated steps:

1. Live worthily.
2. Seek the Spirit earnestly.
3. Recognize spiritual promptings.
4. Respond appropriately.

Seek. Recognize. Respond. It helps to start with small and simple things. Establish a pattern. Get some daily spiritual exercise!

Elder Boyd K. Packer has counseled us to seek the spirit of personal revelation through study and prayer: "Prayer is *your* personal key to heaven. The lock is on your side of the veil."

And how do we recognize spiritual promptings when they do come? Elder Packer acknowledges that describing the promptings from the Holy Ghost to one who has not had them is very difficult. He comments:

"The Holy Ghost speaks with a voice that you *feel* more than you *hear*. It is described as a 'still small voice.'. . . This voice of the Spirit speaks gently, prompting you what to do or what to say, or it may caution or warn you. . . .

"The flow of revelation depends on your faith. You exercise faith by causing, or by making, your mind accept or believe as truth that which *you* cannot, by reason alone, prove for certainty.

"The first exercising of your faith should be your acceptance of Christ and His atonement.

"As you test gospel principles by believing without knowing, the Spirit will begin to teach you. Gradually your faith will be replaced with knowledge.

"You will be able to discern, or to *see*, with spiritual eyes" (*Ensign*, November 1994, p. 60).

Once we've become accustomed to asking the Lord for personal revelation, how do we know that what we feel isn't just ourselves and our own fervent desires speaking? How can we tell the difference between psychological self-deception, wishful thinking, and the promptings of the Holy Ghost?

Elder Packer continues:

"'There are many spirits which are false spirits' (D&C 50:2). There can be counterfeit revelations, promptings from the devil, temptations! . . .

"The seventh chapter of Moroni in the Book of Mormon tells you how to test spiritual promptings. Read it carefully—over and over.

"By trial, and some error, you will learn to heed these promptings.

"If ever you receive a prompting to do something that makes you *feel* uneasy, something you know in your *mind* to be wrong and contrary to the principles of righteousness, do not respond to it!" (*Ensign*, November 1994, p. 61; italics in original).

Self-deception may feel good initially, but deep inside us a nagging whisper of doubt remains. I'm convinced of that. The prophet Isaiah made a wonderful promise to ancient Israel that I firmly believe holds equally true for us today: "And thine ears shall hear a word behind thee, saying, This is the way, walk ye in it, when ye turn to the right hand, and when ye turn to the left" (Isaiah 30:21).

Sometimes just taking "time out" and distancing ourselves from our intense desires will reveal them for what they are: self-deception and "counterfeit revelation." On other occasions we may succeed in temporarily convincing ourselves that our own inner desires are in fact the Lord's will. If those impressions are self-generated and wrong, our inner spiritual sense of "rightness" usually reasserts itself.

If we will but listen, we can hear the Spirit gently prompting us, "*This* is the way! Walk ye in it."

Chapter 10

Examples of the Believers

After my baptism, the remainder of the summer passed swiftly. I could hardly wait until the professor and his family returned so I could share my newfound joy with them. The day after they arrived back in Palo Alto, I drove to their home unannounced and rang the doorbell. The youngest boy opened the door. His eyes widened as his mouth formed an 'O' of surprise.

Then he got so excited he abruptly slammed the door right in my face. I heard him shout, "Mommy! Tish's mommy is here!"

His mother came to the door laughing, "Well, let's at least remember our manners and let her in!"

I couldn't even wait until we sat down. "I've joined the Church!" I announced proudly to the family.

They were momentarily stunned. "Which church? Do you mean *our* church?"

"Of course! The Church of Jesus Christ of Latter-day Saints," I replied with a broad grin.

"How? When? Why?" the questions peppered me from all sides along with hugs and expressions of delight.

"I was baptized about a month ago," I answered as we all plopped down around the kitchen table. In between bites of freshly baked bread slathered with homemade jam, I told them the whole episode.

They were enthralled as I related my experiences, beginning with what a strong positive example and influence their father had been to all the medical students as well as to me personally. We alternately laughed and wept together as I recounted those intensely emotional memories. Now I understood what Dr. Axelrod from my high school science days had said so long ago: The only way to recapture the initial thrill of discovering something truly special is to help someone else find the same wonderful thing.

I remarked, "You know, one of the most interesting things is that finding the Church didn't really seem like a new discovery after all. It was more like recognizing something I'd already known for a long time. I know the gospel is true," I concluded simply.

They nodded their understanding as several of the family members added personal expressions of testimony. While we were talking, I noticed that the professor's face briefly clouded. He actually looked a bit uncomfortable. But after a moment's hesitation he cleared his voice and smiled. "I think this calls for a celebration," he announced. "Let's all go out for ice cream. Tish too!"

With whoops of delight, the children dashed for the car. Tish eagerly bounded along behind them, wagging her tail furiously and barking happily with all the excitement.

Several years later, after I had completed postgraduate training and moved to Salt Lake City, we all had a wonderfully warm reunion and were recounting that joyous first celebration together.

"I remember," one of the older children recalled, "Johnny got so excited he slammed the door right in Annie's face!"

"Tish ate my ice cream cone!"

"We're all related now anyway," Johnny declared. "That's 'cause we have one of Tish's puppies!"

"We named our dog after Tish. We call her 'Tisha,' for 'More-tisha'! Get it?" one of the younger children put in as the others laughed.

"I know," I replied. "Someone else had a 'Paula,' for 'Poli-Tisha'! If your Tisha had puppies herself I suppose one of these days we could also have a 'Reppy,' for 'Repe-Tisha'!"

The children howled with glee at the thought.

The professor smiled indulgently, then grew serious. "Annie, I've always felt just a bit guilty about my possible role in your joining the Church."

"Guilty? Why would you feel guilty?" I asked.

"Well," he replied slowly, "I worried that you may have thought I was something I'm really not."

I was puzzled. "What do you mean?"

"I suppose what I'm trying to say is that I've never thought of myself as what you might call a Model Mormon."

"You were a *wonderful* role model," I protested vehemently.

He shook his head. "That's a separate issue, I think. I try hard to do the right thing. I'm not always completely successful. But what I really mean is something quite different. I guess I've never felt like I'm truly in the 'mainstream' of the Church. Since I've been young I've always had a lot of questions."

I started to comment but he stopped me. "I've never been what you might call the 'ten toes and both hands hangin' on the iron rod' kind of Mormon," he admitted. "I've been concerned that you might have thought I was, well, perhaps more, uh, 'ortho-dox' than I really am."

"I guess I understand what you're saying," I replied. "But let me ask you this: Do you believe that Jesus Christ is the Savior and Redeemer of the world?"

"Of course," he replied immediately.

"Was Joseph Smith a prophet of God?"

"Yes."

"Is the Book of Mormon truly scripture? Do you believe the gospel is true?"

"Yes to both," he said, smiling patiently at the continued questioning.

"Is the Church the Lord's true church?"

He didn't hesitate. "Yes, it is. And the basic gospel principles and doctrines aren't a concern. But," he added as I held my breath and waited for a major-league *but*, "sometimes I feel like I'm an outsider in my own church. I was born and raised in Utah. But somehow I never quite 'fit in' to the local culture. I suppose some people even regarded me as a bit of a maverick."

"First of all," I said, "I don't think there really is such a thing as a 'Model Mormon.' Or a 'Typical Mormon.' Or even an 'Average Mormon.' If someone has faith, believes the gospel fundamentals, loves the Lord, and is keeping His commandments, that's enough for me. What better example could anyone have?"

He didn't answer so I continued, "One of my favorite scriptures is in Second Corinthians, where Paul talks about writing our 'epistles' not with ink or stone tablets but with our hearts and actions that can be 'read' by others. Sort of a 'living testimony.' As I remember, you never said a word about the Church to me. You simply lived what you believe. After all, we're told, 'by their fruits shall ye know them.'"

He sighed with evident relief. "Well, thank you. I just didn't want you to think I was something I really wasn't. I'm glad you found the Church and the gospel and that I may have had some small part in that process of discovery."

Many people share my friend's concerns. No one wants to feel like a hypocrite. But being a hypocrite means professing or pretending to be something we really aren't. It is normal to feel inadequate, particularly when measured against the seemingly impossible goal of perfection. Recognizing our limitations and shortcomings is clearly essential for our eternal progression. However, we must avoid the spiritual paralysis that can sometimes result from dwelling on those inadequacies. After all, perfection is not just an eternal goal, it's a process. We are counseled to "continue in patience until [we] are perfected" (D&C 67:13).

The scriptures also tell us that being perfect does not necessarily mean being without flaw or blemish. Read the footnote to Matthew 5:48. The Greek word translated as *perfect* actually means "complete, finished, fully developed." The Lord expects us to be working toward perfection; he doesn't expect us to attain it instantaneously!

The Lord has further commanded us to be examples of the 'believers' and to let our light shine before men. Actions do speak louder than words. Fortunately for me, most of the Latter-day Saints I first encountered were wonderful representatives of their faith, even if they were not perfect ones.

As the weeks after my baptism swiftly passed, I knew I had made the right decision. It felt good. It also seemed as though—in a figurative yet eternal sense—I had indeed come Home.

For the most part, the ward members made me feel welcome and wanted. Not unexpectedly, there were a few rough spots. One such experience is a vivid memory, even twenty-five years later. In retrospect it seems inconsequential and insignificant, even rather silly. But at the time it was a big deal.

During the first two years of medical school, the students dressed very casually; jeans and T-shirts were the accepted norm. I appreciated the relaxed atmosphere but also always enjoyed wearing nice clothes for special occasions. And for me, church was a very special occasion indeed.

To put one of my postbaptismal "downers" in context, remember that the 'sixties were the first real miniskirt era. Although the extreme "micro minis" frankly never appealed to me, I did wear my skirts a fashionable but comparatively modest (at least by the standards of the time) two or three inches above the kneecap. My absolute favorite outfit was a rose-colored skirt with matching vest that I wore with a pale pink, long-sleeved silk shirt. A patterned scarf knotted around my neck and fastened with a gold pin complemented the ensemble. When I wore that outfit I felt especially sharp.

Without thinking about it, I wore the favored outfit to church a couple of times. The second time, one of the sisters in the ward drew me aside after Sunday School. "Sister Osborn," she said in an intense near-whisper, "I need to talk with you. *Now!*"

Wondering at the urgency in her voice, I followed her into the relative privacy of the women's rest room.

"Some of the other sisters and I think you need a bit of friendly advice," she stated. "They don't want to hurt your feelings so they won't say anything to you. But I will. And I'm going to."

Instinctively I braced myself. She slowly looked me up and down, sending an unspoken message by letting her eyes deliberately linger on the hem of my skirt. I flushed under her scrutiny, suddenly understanding what was coming.

"Your skirts are way too short," she said in a flat, somewhat judgmental tone. "You would *never* be allowed into a Mutual dance," she continued, referring to the events held occasionally for the stake's young men and women. "Certainly not dressed like *that*! You know what they do at those dances?"

I shook my head silently.

"If a young woman comes in a short skirt, they make her kneel on the floor. If her hem doesn't touch the floor, they send her straight home!" she concluded dramatically.

I was outraged just thinking about such embarrassment. A spectrum of heated responses flashed through my mind, with "It's none of your business" and "I'd never want to go to one of those dances anyway" right at the top of the list.

I said none of them. I glared at her for a long moment, gritting my teeth. Finally I just said stonily, "Thank you for your interest and concern," and stalked out of the rest room.

The more I thought about that encounter, the madder I became. In retrospect I realize that my emotionally charged reaction was caused by more than the acute humiliation of the moment. The episode made me feel like an ugly duckling all over again.

I was really steamed. I felt personally offended. I even savored the delicious feeling of righteous indignation to which I felt quite justifiably entitled.

I stewed about the incident for several days. I formulated several possible responses, ranging from talking to the bishop to leaving the Church in a huff—or just walking away quietly and never going back.

In the end, I did none of the above.

I swallowed my pride. Instead of tripping over that stumbling block, I stepped over it and lengthened my stride. And my skirts.

Why? Once the anger and heat of the moment dissipated, I tried to put the unfortunate event in perspective. Admittedly, it wasn't easy. My pride had indeed been wounded. But I knew the

Church was true. Could I allow the well-intentioned but tactless, insensitive behavior of one member distract me from that central fact? No way! The Church was a great blessing in my life and I knew it. I decided to let the incident drop. I couldn't forget but I could certainly forgive.

From that seemingly trivial but nonetheless difficult personal experience I learned another component of what would later become the Simeon Solution:

3. Focus on the fundamentals.

If we strive earnestly to remain focused, rooted, centered, and grounded in basic gospel principles, then personalities and peripheral issues will neither confuse nor distract us from our eternal goals.

A verse from a favorite Latter-day Saint hymn comes to mind:

> *Be fixed in your purpose, for Satan will try you;*
> *The weight of your calling he perfectly knows.*
> *Your path may be thorny, but Jesus is nigh you;*
> *His arm is sufficient, tho demons oppose.*
> "The Time Is Far Spent" (*Hymns*, no. 266)

To remain fixed in our purpose requires perspective, determination, and maturity. It often takes real work. But if we can adopt Simeon's sound attitude of patience and trust, then personal disappointments and unresolved issues can be appropriately and successfully placed on a spiritual "back burner."

It makes me shudder to think what would have happened—or, perhaps more accurately, *not* happened—if I had stalked out of the Church in offense twenty-five years ago.

Chapter 11

Setback

It was simply too wonderful an opportunity to pass up. London in the middle of an English winter wasn't particularly inviting, but the chance to spend two months learning pediatrics at the famed Hospital for Sick Children was irresistible. Also intriguing was the opportunity to attend my newfound church outside the U.S.A. Would it be as appealing as my beloved Palo Alto Stake? Recalling Max's promises, I expected it would be.

One of the families who had been instrumental in my post-baptismal fellowshipping knew a young couple who had just completed graduate school at Stanford, then moved to London where the husband was employed as the local representative of an American company. Concerned that I would arrive in London and need to search for housing in the dead of winter, my friends wrote the young couple and asked if I could stay with them for a few days while I settled in. I was relieved at their prompt reply, extending a warm invitation to share their small but cozy suburban flat for a few days after my arrival.

London in late February was as advertised: cold, damp, and dark with leaden, smoky-gray skies. But the small flat bustled with warmth and activity. A glowing coal fire in the grate radiated cheer that was exceeded only by the welcome from my hostess. She was a bright, very attractive woman about my own age. Obviously delighted to have an American visitor, even a thoroughly jet-lagged one, she gave me a big hug. Before bustling me off to bed, she sat me down for a glass of milk and a plate of cookies freshly baked with some of her precious supply of chocolate chips imported from home.

The young couple had three beautiful, extremely lively children. The oldest, a somewhat solemn, serious five year old, and the middle child, an irrepressible and mischievous two year old, were excited at the prospect of a brand-new source of play and entertainment. Their mother, occupied with a new baby, clearly welcomed the diversion.

We settled into an easy routine. I worked at the hospital and searched for housing during the day, then returned via the "tube" at dusk. Pam and I chatted amicably together as we fixed the evening meals, washed and folded laundry, entertained the older children, and fed the baby. It was my first in-depth look at the inner workings of a young Latter-day Saint family. I liked what I saw.

Except for one thing: Pam's husband, Paul.

Paul was an intelligent but aloof man who maintained his office in their home, consulting and rendering advice via telephone and mail. Other than an occasional foray into outlying areas to conduct site visits and negotiations for his company, his schedule was light and largely self-imposed, leaving moderate blocks of time unoccupied. He had carefully positioned a worn but comfortable easy chair and ottoman in the office, where he often sat and read while Pam struggled alone with the three children.

My puzzlement must have been apparent.

"Anne, you're wondering why I don't help Pam," he said.

Caught. I nodded.

"You're new in the Church. You obviously have a lot to learn," he said archly. "One of those things is the proper role and place of women."

The clear implication was that I was seriously deficient in that understanding.

"I'm the provider. I earn the living for this family. It's also my role as the priesthood holder to preside over the family and instruct my wife and children. It's my wife's role to bear our children, do the housework, and take care of the children. That's the way it is in our home. And frankly, that's the way it should be," he stated flatly. "The proper place for a woman is on a well-worn path between the kitchen and the bedroom!"

I laughed, thinking he was joking. He wasn't. His look of stern rebuke silenced me. Paul was totally serious, completely convinced of his moral rectitude. To him, the priesthood seemed to be a license to rule, not a commitment and obligation to serve.

Paul also regarded himself as quite a scriptorian and an expert in Church history. He delighted in expounding on obscure points of doctrine, most of which were completely unfamiliar to me. I suppose it was a bizarre, rather juvenile way of showing off and demonstrating his intellectual superiority.

A convert of only a few months, I was still "wet behind the ears." I was also in the process of reading the scriptures, further digesting and assimilating basic gospel principles. When I wanted to discuss simple, uncomplicated fundamentals, he acted bored and digressed, quoting extensively from the *Journal of Discourses,* the King Follett sermon, and relatively obscure secondary sources to substantiate his own interpretations.

It was confusing. I felt frustrated and discouraged, even somewhat disillusioned. Was Pam's husband really the Model Mormon Male he held himself out to be? Or was he an aberration, someone who wrested the scriptures and doctrines to suit his own personal needs and justify his arrogant behavior? Somewhat diffidently, I asked Pam about it.

"Oh," she replied with remarkable equanimity, "that's just Paul. Down deep he really is basically a good guy. I've learned to live with it."

I could never do that, I thought. *Not in a million years.*

Shortly afterward I found a place to live near the hospital and moved out. Periodically during my two months in London I thought about Pam and her husband. I wished I could discuss the issue with my Mormon friends in California, but they were five thousand miles away.

Studying the scriptures helped. When I read D&C 121 for the first time, it became readily apparent what proper exercise of priesthood authority really means. According to the revelation received by the Prophet Joseph Smith when he was in Liberty jail, many are called but few are chosen.

"And why are they not chosen? . . . they do not learn this one lesson—

"That the rights of the priesthood are inseparably connected with the powers of heaven, and that the powers of heaven cannot be controlled nor handled only upon the principles of righteousness.

"That they may be conferred upon us, it is true; but when we undertake to cover our sins, or to gratify our pride, our vain ambition, *or to exercise control or dominion or compulsion upon the souls of the children of men, in any degree of unrighteousness* . . . the Spirit of the Lord is grieved; and when it is withdrawn, *Amen to the priesthood or the authority of that man*" (D&C 121:34–37; italics added).

Reading that scripture, I felt reassured and comforted. When I finally returned to Stanford, I told my friends about Pam's husband and his attitudes, which seemed such a contrast to their own gentle examples.

One of the men had been Paul's bishop. "I was afraid of that," he sighed resignedly. "Paul has always been convinced he knew the 'right' way things should be done. I was hoping that over the years he had mellowed."

He grinned wryly as he continued, "I guess there are some real male chauvinists in the world. A few are also members of the Church. We're not immune. It's unfortunate but true: Such people misinterpret the scriptures and use priesthood authority as an excuse to justify their own selfish actions."

He then added some terrifically sound advice. "Don't let someone else's inconsiderate or even inappropriate conduct become your own problem. Such people will eventually answer to the Lord for their actions. That's their problem, not yours."

I nodded silently in agreement, remembering the Skirt Incident.

All of us may encounter someone or something that seems jarringly inconsistent or incompatible with the basic principles and spirit of the gospel. It may be a disturbing concept or the less-than-ideal personal example of another Church member. The scriptures and basic teachings of the prophets provide a sure, eternal standard by which such experiences can be judged. Thoughtful study of those sources together with earnest prayer usually resolves the issue.

President Howard W. Hunter has strongly emphasized the importance of using gentle persuasion, not coercion, in exercising personal agency:

"God's chief way of acting is by persuasion and patience and long-suffering, not by coercion and stark confrontation. He acts by gentle solicitation and by sweet enticement. He always acts with unfailing respect for the freedom and independence that we possess. He wants to help us and pleads for the chance to assist us, but he will not do so in violation of our agency. . . .

"To countermand and ultimately forbid our choices was Satan's way, not God's, and the Father of us all simply never will do that. He will, however, stand by us forever to help us see the right path, find the right choice, respond to the true voice, and feel the influence of his undeniable Spirit. His gentle, peaceful, powerful persuasion to do right and find joy will be with us 'so long as time shall last, or the earth shall stand, or there shall be one man upon the face thereof to be saved.' (Moro. 7:36)" (*Ensign,* August 1994, back cover).

Whether favorable or unfavorable, personal examples should not determine our own response to the Church and the gospel. My medical school professor was a wonderful example, but I didn't join the Church because of him. Pam's husband was (at least in my opinion) a rather poor example, but I didn't leave the Church because of him, either. I'm glad, too! If I had permitted that episode to overwhelm my testimony of the gospel's truthfulness, I would never have experienced the joy that my future experiences in the Church would bring so abundantly.

Another fundamental principle of the Simeon Solution was thus added:

4. Stand firm in the faith.

In his address at the 1994 General Relief Society Meeting, President Hunter counseled Latter-day Saint women to "stand firm in the faith," citing Nephi's statement, "Ye must press forward with a steadfastness in Christ, having a perfect brightness of hope, and a love of God and of all men" (2 Nephi 31:20).

The Church is true. We should also be true to the Church. Fidelity and loyalty, virtues that are often in short supply in modern society, are indeed their own rewards.

The Lord blesses those who stand firm in the faith and diligently keep his commandments. I was about to find out just how wonderful those blessings can be.

Chapter 12

Single and Sane Simultaneously?

If I heard it once, I heard it a thousand times. In fact, it got to be downright annoying. A well-meaning member, ironically often an older sister, would draw me aside and inquire solicitously, "Sister Osborn, why aren't you married yet?" With the bolder women it was more like a statement, "You know, if you were really doing what the Lord wanted you to do, you'd be married and having babies!"

I didn't want to be rude (well, at least not *really* rude). But it was actually none of their business. So, depending on my mood and the level of their intrusiveness, I would sometimes ask innocently, "Why do you want to know?" That usually elicited a flustered stammer, "Well, uh, I guess I was just curious." Then I wouldn't say another word. At other times I assumed a very woebegone expression and replied sadly, "Well, no one has ever asked me." *That* response often caused a blush of embarrassment as the nosy questioner beat a hasty exit!

The truth of the matter is, I worried about it myself. Trying to remain gospel centered and sane while being single in an avowedly married church isn't an easy job. (As a matter of fact, being married with a family isn't so easy either, but that's another story.)

I often silently asked, *If it's so important, why haven't I gotten married yet?* Was it, as some suggested none too delicately, that perhaps I was "too picky"? Others, even less diplomatic, said I probably "intimidated the socks off" any potential suitors! I was certainly trying hard to keep the commandments. So where were the promised blessings I felt I was due? After all, as the scriptures clearly state, "I, the Lord, am bound when ye do what I say; but when ye do not what I say, ye have no promise" (D&C 82:10).

I entreated the Lord. Then nagged him. No answer. It took quite a while—with much thought, prayer, study, and not a small amount of anguish—before I got the whole issue in proper perspective.

Doctors sometimes wryly joke that the most powerful diagnostic instrument known to man is the "retrospectoscope." As in, "In retrospect, this patient's symptoms first began . . ." or, "In retrospect, the first time the patient's lung cancer could be identified on chest X-ray was . . ."

I applied a spiritual retrospectoscope to my own situation. As I reflected back on the defining moments in my life, it was as plain as day that the Lord had guided those pivotal choices. He was aware of my needs long before I recognized them, before I even acknowledged his presence and influence. He took care of me then; why doubt him now? Yes, I was disappointed that some anticipated blessings hadn't materialized. But in many other respects, I felt blessed beyond my wildest hopes.

I finally realized that the rhythm and pace, the "times and seasons," of each individual's life are different. The critical thing is to discover what our own times and seasons are and to make the most of them, not yearn to follow someone else's timetable. *Heavenly Father has a plan,* not just for his children collectively but for each one of us individually.

Patience is a virtue I still find in short supply, at least in my own life. I still struggle with the temptation to prescribe how and especially *when* (usually sooner, not later!) I want those promised blessings to occur. In retrospect, I'm profoundly grateful that in his infinite love the Lord hasn't always given me what I desired but instead has blessed me with what he knew I needed!

Once again, the scriptures provide wisdom and perspective: "Wait on the Lord: be of good courage, and he shall strengthen thine heart: wait, I say, on the Lord" (Psalm 27:14).

Going to the temple also helped me gain much-needed perspective. I had been a member of the Church for about five years when my convert brother and sister-in-law were ready to receive their endowments in the Oakland Temple. Our bishop felt I was also ready, so after careful preparation the three of us went together.

Thoughtful preparation, growing spiritual maturity, and attitude make the essential difference in individual response to the temple endowment. For me, going to the temple was an incredibly rich spiritual blessing. The temple workers were serious but kind and solicitous. The doctrines were pure, the teachings clear, the covenants meaningful, and the promised blessings unambiguous.

My temple experience and study of the scriptures helped me learn two more essential aspects of the Simeon Solution:

5. *Be patient.*
6. *Adopt the eternal perspective.*

Like Simeon, we need to be patient, remain faithful, and wait for fulfillment of the Lord's promises to be given in the Lord's own time. The temple experience helped me understand that no blessing essential for our happiness and eternal progression will be denied, if we are faithful and obedient. It just may not come as soon as we might wish!

91

However, maintaining that eternal perspective isn't always easy. At least it wasn't for me. Because my schedule was so irregular, I lived alone. When I came home after a long and exhausting day at the hospital, my home was always dark and silent. I had no one with whom to share the frustrations and disappointments of a difficult day.

Except Tish, of course. Somehow sensing those rough times when I felt isolated and achingly alone, she would shove her muzzle under my arm and whimper softly in sympathy. Her tail would thump the floor as if to say, "Please don't worry. It's okay. I'm here. Everything's going to be all right."

Canine comfort was wonderful, but it was no substitute for the real thing, the eternal companionship described in the scriptures. Attending the temple sealings of friends and neighbors was always a poignant, sweet-sad experience for me.

Holidays were especially hard during those long years I was single. For some people Christmas is a particularly difficult time. The sense of heightened expectation, the joyous, upbeat atmosphere, the family gatherings all accentuate already painful feelings of loneliness and isolation.

For me, Mothers' Day was by far the worst. The absolute pits. I dutifully sat through interminable programs as the Primary children sang to harried yet proud mothers. I winced inwardly as all the mothers in the congregation were asked to rise and receive a small gift, usually a potted plant or modest corsage. It always seemed as though I was the only woman who wasn't standing and smiling. Instead I slouched down in the pew, feeling different, left out, and even a bit ashamed.

I started skipping church on Mothers' Day. It wasn't the right thing to do, of course. In fact, it made me feel quite guilty and disloyal, but feeling guilty seemed much better than feeling like an ugly duckling. Either way, it hurt, and hurt a lot. (It wasn't until many years later when a sensitive bishop decided it was appropriate to honor *all* the adult women of the ward—single, married with children, married but childless, divorced, and widowed—that I resumed going to church on Mothers' Day.)

The remainder of my medical training at Stanford was a blur of tireless study, sleepless nights, and endless examinations. But I finished it. Specialty certification finally in hand (thirteen years of relentless, highly competitive education after high school) I left California for my first real job: Instructor of Radiology at the University of Utah School of Medicine.

I did look forward to enjoying the single social scene in Utah. Everyone had warned me that the ratio of single men to single women in Salt Lake City was far from promising. But compared to Palo Alto, it seemed like a veritable Promised Land. In California I had known almost no worthy, tithe-paying, temple-going, single Latter-day Saint men in their thirties. Or forties. Or (gulp) even their fifties.

After arriving in Salt Lake City I dated what seemed like nearly every eligible bachelor between Logan and Springville, Maine to Montana. Enduring innumerable dates and even some euphemistically termed "Special Interest" events seemed a small price to pay for the possibility of an eternal companionship and the blessing of celestial marriage.

It didn't happen.

Thirty-one passed in a flash. Thirty-two. Thirty-five. The years inexorably rolled by. Good ones. Lonely ones. Despite my best intentions, I still sometimes nagged the Lord. And I almost—but not quite—got married.

I finally decided that one very nice, soft-spoken widower came reasonably close to what I thought was desirable in an eternal companion. He was considerably older than I, but from the eternal perspective that really doesn't count for much, does it? When he asked me to marry him, I hesitated only because I hadn't received the strong spiritual confirmation that had accompanied other truly crucial decisions in my life.

I put him off. Frustrated, he began pressing for an answer. So, in fasting and prayer, I finally went to the temple. After the session was finished I sat in the celestial room for what seemed like hours, entreating the Lord to reveal his will. Should my answer be "yes," "no," or perhaps "I'm still not sure"?

Cosmic silence.

I had temporarily forgotten a fundamental lesson from the scriptures that I had learned years before as an investigator. As if through a still, small voice this scripture came to mind: "Behold, you have not understood; you have supposed that I would give it unto you, when you took no thought save it was to ask me.

"But, behold, I say unto you, that you must study it out in your mind; then you must ask me if it be right, and if it is right I will cause that your bosom shall burn within you; therefore, you shall feel that it is right" (D&C 9:7–8).

Impatient, I finally said to the Lord, "Well, I've made up my mind. I'm going to do it. I'm going to marry Brother _____. If I'm right, please let me feel peace about it. And if I'm not, *please* let me know."

The ensuing reply was a single firm but powerful mental "*No!*" The impression was so strong it almost seemed auditory. Startled at the strength of the unexpected answer, I looked up and said out loud, "*What?*" Gently shushed by a nearby temple worker, I repeated the inquiry and received the same impression.

I'm chagrined and embarrassed to admit it, but I didn't actually believe the answer. I thought my vivid imagination was working overtime. I left the temple intending to accept the proposal. Still somewhat uncertain about my decision, I dismissed my nagging anxieties. I temporarily succeeded in suppressing the uncomfortable feeling that something wasn't quite right. But however much I tried, those uncomfortable sensations would not disappear completely.

The afternoon of the next day, a bright and beautiful Sabbath, I was quietly reading when someone knocked at the front door. I peeked out the window and was surprised to see one of the priesthood leaders in our stake standing on the doorstep. He told me he was out walking in the neighborhood and thought he'd drop by "just to see how I was doing."

It was odd. Definitely odd. I had seen his wife out walking briskly on many occasions, but never her husband. This good man is a modest, rather diffident person. So when he came in and sat down in the living room, he was understandably somewhat uncomfortable and ill at ease.

After a few halting, desultory comments, he finally cleared his throat and came to the point. "I suppose I'd better tell you why I came by," he began with some hesitation. "Last night I just couldn't get to sleep. So after tossing and turning for a while I finally gave up. I went downstairs into the study to read and ponder the scriptures. After a while I began meditating, then praying, pouring my heart out to the Lord in gratitude for his mercy and blessings. At that moment I think I felt closer to the Lord than at any other time in my life. The veil seemed so thin it was as though I could almost reach through it."

He paused at the vivid memory, then continued, "The Lord made some things known to me, personal things about some events that would take place in my life later on. Then at the end of my prayer, something quite unusual happened. I began to think about you. And I had the unmistakable impression that you were facing a critical decision in your life. I wasn't told what it was. No details. But what I *was* told by the Spirit is that you were about to make the wrong choice. Whatever that is," he smiled almost apologetically, "you're supposed to say no!"

I was stunned. How could he possibly have known?

"Well, actually . . . I *am* in a real quandary about something very important," I admitted. Then I corrected myself, "I mean I *was* in a quandary. I was going to say 'yes' when I know I should say 'no.' Not to anything bad," I added hastily. "Now I know what I need to do."

So I turned down the proposal. But it would be years before I would know how right that decision was.

I learned an important lesson from that experience. When we plead with the Lord for help, *the answer to our prayers often comes through another individual.* It has been said that answers to prayer usually don't come down through the roof but they do come knocking on the door! The corollary is that we should strive to be spiritually in tune so that, should he choose, the Lord can use us to bless the lives of others.

The first time such an opportunity came to me, I'm sorry to report I ignored it.

Toward the end of my medical training, I had the opportunity to study for a few months with a particularly outstanding professor in North Carolina. I moved into a spartan but clean apartment within easy driving distance of the medical center.

Busy with the added studies, I usually worked long hours and finished late. Regarding myself as a temporary resident, I didn't make much effort to interact with the other tenants in our modest apartment complex. But I did come to know a divorced woman who lived in a crowded one-bedroom unit with her two young boys.

One night as I was driving home, I had the distinct impression that I should stop off and visit with that struggling young mother. Somehow I felt she was in trouble. But I was tired. Too busy. I was preoccupied with studying for the terrifying specialty board examinations that loomed just a few weeks away. I ignored the feelings, ate a makeshift dinner, and went to bed.

The next evening the feelings returned, stronger and more persistent. I ignored them again, attributing them to my imagination.

I woke up the next morning with the nagging, insistent feeling that something was really wrong. She *did* need my help. I had an early case scheduled at the hospital so I couldn't see her then. But the evening would be soon enough, I thought.

I worried about it all day. The sense of foreboding was overpowering. As soon as I could, I rushed back and hurried over to her apartment.

Empty.

The dingy curtains were drawn back, revealing a silent room. The battered, nicked furniture was scattered in disarray. A broken toy lay abandoned on the worn carpet.

Gulping back tears, I banged insistently on the door of the adjacent apartment. A woman dressed in an old housecoat and bedroom slippers answered, a cigarette dangling from her lip.

"Where's Vicky?" I demanded breathlessly, fearing the answer.

"Ah dunno," she replied laconically. "She packed up the kids and left this morning. Took off like she was in one heck of a big hurry."

"Where'd she go?"

The woman shrugged. "Dunno. She never tol' nobody. She was closemouthed, that one."

My shoulders sagged in defeat and I turned slowly back toward my own small apartment.

To this day, I don't know what happened to Vicky and her children. What I *do* know is that I somehow failed her and disappointed the Lord. I hope against hope that someone else more responsive to the Spirit stepped forward to help.

It's easy to offer a smooth litany of excuses. Too busy. Too tired. Too preoccupied. Too distracted. But when we ourselves need help, we hope fervently that someone else will be listening attentively and responsively for those spiritual promptings. As for me, I promised the Lord I would never ignore them again.

Vicky, wherever you are, I'm sorry. I hope things worked out. I learned my lesson. I just hope the cost to you wasn't too high.

Chapter 13

Obedience

The air of anticipation that filled the stake center was almost palpable. The excited young women chatted animatedly with their mothers as they began filling the chapel more than an hour before the scheduled meeting time. The group rapidly overflowed into the adjacent cultural hall as numerous rows of folding chairs were removed from storage and hurriedly set up.

This particular Young Women's conference was a truly special occasion in our stake. One of the Twelve Apostles had accepted the invitation to address the girls, their mothers, and the ward and stake auxiliary leaders. The stake presidency, stake high council, and bishoprics were seated on the stand with the Young Women leaders. I felt especially privileged to be present in the congregation as the adopted "big sister" of some neighbors in the stake.

The buzz of conversation hushed abruptly as the presiding Apostle was escorted to the podium. After the welcome, opening hymn, invocation, and a special musical number, the Young Women's president and our stake president each spoke briefly.

At last, the long-awaited moment arrived. There was an audible rustle as the Apostle was introduced. He arranged his scriptures on the podium and adjusted his glasses. He warmly acknowledged the stake officers and graciously thanked the young women for this special opportunity to address them.

"My dear young sisters," he began as he took out his written talk. Then he suddenly stopped, staring intently at the unfolded pages. He took a deep breath and momentarily closed his eyes. When he finally opened them, he smiled faintly and nodded slightly as if to himself.

With a small sigh he carefully refolded the talk and put it back inside his coat pocket. "Dear sisters," he began again, "I had a talk all prepared. But the talk I'd prepared for you isn't the one the Lord wants me to give now. I feel prompted to speak about an entirely different subject."

You could have heard a pin drop.

"A few days ago I received a letter written by several girls who were roommates at BYU. It was two pages full of single-spaced typewritten questions. The questions dealt very specifically and in rather graphic clinical detail with a variety of dating situations. The bottom line is that they wanted to know just how far they could go and still stay morally clean."

He grinned ruefully. "To tell you the truth, I had absolutely no idea how to begin answering them. The questions started with a first date and ran all the way to if you were engaged how intimate you could be and still maintain temple worthiness.

"I hate to admit it," he continued, "but I procrastinated answering them. I put that letter on the very bottom of my correspondence pile and tried to forget about it."

We all smiled, knowing how easy it is to procrastinate.

"After a few days, the letter gradually worked its way to the top of the pile. I still didn't know what to do with it. So I put it right back on the bottom again!"

An audible chuckle from the audience punctuated his remarks.

He peered over his glasses at the group. "When the letter resurfaced the second time, I knew I had to do something about it. But I still had no idea how to approach answering their questions. So finally I went to the temple in fasting and prayer. I asked the Lord how I could help these sisters. And then the answer came to me, clearly and unambiguously. With a grateful and relieved heart I returned to the office and began dictating my long-delayed reply."

He grew serious. "I said, 'Dear Sisters: The problem is you're asking the wrong questions. The question isn't how close you can come to the edge of the cliff before falling off, but how far away can you stay!'"

When I heard that statement, I had the satisfying inward *aha!* of discovery. For sure, I thought, no one ever fell off a cliff who didn't get close enough to get pushed over the edge or, peering into the abyss below, get spiritual vertigo and lose balance.

Few of us are ever dragged kicking and screaming to the precipice and bodily thrown over the edge! More commonly, we succumb to curiosity, gradually creeping toward the cliff to see what's there. Or we experiment with just how close to the edge we can walk without falling off.

The Apostle elaborated this concept further, illustrating how important it is not merely to obey the commandments but to observe them with exactness. He taught that diligent, willing obedience is absolutely crucial for our eternal progression. His counsel was to avoid compromising situations, staying as far away as possible from potential temptation or even the appearance of wrongdoing.

I've never forgotten that talk and the profound impact it had on everyone present. It became another guiding principle of the Simeon Solution:

7. *Keep the commandments.*

Grudging, reluctant, or fearful obedience is not sufficient. Helaman attributed the success of his outnumbered stripling warriors to their obedience, faith, and trust in the Lord: "They did obey and observe to perform every word of command *with exactness;* yea, and even according to their faith it was done unto them" (Alma 57:21; italics added).

Likewise, the Lord commanded Joshua: "Only be thou strong and very courageous, that thou mayest observe to do according to all the law, which Moses my servant commanded thee: turn not from it to the right hand or to the left, that thou mayest prosper whithersoever thou goest" (Joshua 1:7).

The Lord has said he will bless us if we keep his commandments with exactness, diligence, honor, and a willing spirit. I was about to discover how generously he keeps his end of the bargain!

Chapter 14

Ron

At last I felt genuine peace and contentment. The major, life-changing decisions I had made—sometimes knowingly, sometimes not—seemed to be the right ones. In retrospect, I now realize that the Lord brought me to this place, at this time.

I really liked Salt Lake City and loved our neighborhood with its cozy homes. I enjoyed the ward and felt very much at ease there. Many neighbors included me in family activities, and I developed the custom of inviting widows and families with hard-pressed mothers to Sunday dinner.

My career was also progressing. My first radiology textbook was well under way and I liked teaching in the medical school. Patients with difficult diagnostic problems were often referred to the University Medical Center. Using the combination of medical knowledge and spiritual insight to bless the lives of others was both gratifying and effective.

The prophet Amulek taught the Nephites to exercise faith and call on the Lord to bless their homes and families, their crops and fields (see Alma 34:17–25). Would the same process work with patients? Indeed it did! I found that if I were faced with a genuinely puzzling medical problem, prayer often worked wonders. Following the Lord's admonition to Oliver Cowdery in the ninth section of the Doctrine and Covenants, I would mull over a diagnostic dilemma and "study it out" in my mind, then ask the Lord if the conclusion I had reached was the correct one. If it was right, I felt the confirming influence of the Spirit. Skeptical colleagues wouldn't have believed it. But it worked! I never signed the Lord's name at the bottom of my X-ray reports, but at least *I* knew it belonged there.

I rarely dated now. As the years passed and I reached my mid-thirties, the already narrow "field" of eligible (read: active Latter-day Saint and at least somewhat appealing) men narrowed to a seemingly miniscule number. No matter. I was growing professionally, had a social schedule filled with family and neighborhood activities, and continued to learn about the gospel. I studied Church history and doctrine. I taught evening institute classes on the Book of Mormon and the New Testament.

By this period in my life I really felt I would in all likelihood never marry, at least not in mortality. But that was okay. The Simeon Solution and its eternal perspective made me certain that if I were faithful, no requisite blessings would ultimately be denied me.

I found the words of President Lorenzo Snow, confirmed by many subsequent Church leaders (including President Howard W. Hunter), especially comforting: "There is no Latter-day Saint who dies after having lived a faithful life who will lose anything because of having failed to do certain things when opportunities were not furnished him or her. In other words, if a young man or a young woman has no opportunity of getting married, and they live faithful lives up to the time of their death, they will have all the blessings, exaltation, and glory that any man or woman will have who had this opportunity and improved it. That is sure and positive"

(Clyde J. Williams, comp., *The Teachings of Lorenzo Snow* [Salt Lake City: Bookcraft, 1984], p. 138).

Still more years passed, for the most part happily and productively. After serving for several years on the Sunday School General Board, I was called to serve on the Relief Society General Board.

At April conference in 1981, I was seated with the other auxiliary general board members in the front of the Tabernacle. After one of the sessions had concluded, Elder Ronald E. Poelman of the Seventy came into the congregation and chatted with me briefly. One of his brothers together with his wife and children had been guests at my traditional Sunday dinners. Elder Poelman had seen them recently and came down to convey to me their greetings. We were interrupted mid-conversation by someone who wanted to speak to me about an upcoming regional conference. Elder Poelman turned away, and we didn't speak again for another six months.

I really didn't know Ronald Poelman. He had been a counselor in the Palo Alto stake presidency when I had joined the Church. We had never become personally acquainted, although he later came to know my brother, Greg, who was serving in the bishopric of one of the Stanford wards.

Elder Poelman moved to Utah in 1978 after he was called as a General Authority. His first wife, Claire, died in 1979 after a protracted bout with breast cancer. Elder Poelman, a tall, handsome, but somewhat aloof man had evinced no interest whatsoever in dating. Contrary to popular impression, none of the Brethren ever pressed him to remarry.

At October conference in 1981, he again approached me following the Saturday morning session, this time to convey a greeting from my brother, Greg, whom he had just seen the previous week in California. I looked over Elder Poelman's shoulder and saw most of the Quorum of Seventy along with many of the Twelve intently observing the interchange. Ron later told me (*much* later, I might add!) that he had looked over my shoulder and seen the Relief Society General Board members assiduously trying not to stare at the two of us.

Once more we were interrupted. And once more he turned away. During lunch later that day, Barbara Smith, then general president of the Relief Society, pointedly asked me, "What's this with you and Elder Poelman?"

"What do you mean?"

"Just what I said. I saw you talking together."

I blushed (a rare event for a clinically hardened doctor) and replied somewhat heatedly, "Well, it's nothing. I really don't know him at all."

She persisted, "Well, do you *like* him?"

I was really flustered. "I said I don't *know* him. I've talked with him at general conference. That's all!"

She wouldn't let it drop. "Well, would you like to date him?"

I silently ground my teeth and replied, trying unsuccessfully to terminate the exchange, "If he ever wants to call me, he will. He can look up my number in the Church directory. It's right there."

Barbara's husband, Doug, had been observing this interchange quietly. He finally spoke up and observed, "Annie, it's not that simple. First of all, a General Authority can't just date casually like anyone else. He has no privacy. Second, let me make another observation. If Barbara died and I were single, the mere thought of calling someone—especially someone like you—for a date would terrify me! I'd rather dig a hole, crawl into it, and pull the top over me than pick up that phone. I'd need a bit of encouragement. You can be rather intimidating, you know."

Hmm. Doug Smith was a confident, competent, successful

executive. Perhaps it wasn't as simple as I had naively supposed. And maybe I was somewhat aloof myself, carrying my professional demeanor around as an invisible but definite shield.

I didn't say anything more after that. But I did think about what Brother Smith had said, and I finally decided he was right. Perhaps Elder Poelman needed that bit of encouragement. I called his brother and sister-in-law and invited them for dinner the following Sunday night. When they accepted readily, I called Elder Poelman and asked if he would feel comfortable joining us for a quiet evening. To the surprise of both of us he replied, "Yes. I'd like that."

I've never planned a menu more carefully to seem casual and effortless. And it worked; it *was* a nice evening. Amazingly, it wasn't even awkward. The four of us enjoyed the food and conversation, then washed the dishes and cleaned up the kitchen together. Elder Poelman looked around the house, noting the titles in my extensive library. ("Have you read all those books?" "Not all, but most of them." "Is this your tool kit?" "Yes." "Do you know how to use all those things?" "Yes, most of them." He later said jokingly that *that* was when he really started to get interested.)

Elder Poelman arrived and left with his brother and sister-in-law. Safer that way, I guess! Certainly appropriate. Afterward he wrote me a nice, very proper thank-you note. And I didn't hear from him again for two months.

In early December, his sister-in-law called to invite me to their home for what sounded like a rather unusual evening. Elder Poelman was taking his youngest daughter, Laurel, then a sophomore at BYU, to Israel during the holidays. His brother and sister-in-law planned to show slides of their own trip several years before. Would I like to join them? A strange "date," if that's what it was: inviting someone to see your brother's old slides of his Holy

Land trip! I had already promised friends I would play doubles tennis but agreed to come as soon as we finished.

That evening, hair still wet from a quick shower, I walked the few blocks to their home. Laurel apparently had to cancel at the last minute so the four of us watched the slides and chatted casually. As we were preparing to leave after some light refreshments, Ron noted that the only car outside was his. By then it was cold, the wind was howling, and it was starting to snow. So he did the gracious thing: He asked if he could drive me home.

From his point of view, it was a "white knuckle" trip. And not because the roads were slick with the first dusting of snow, either! When we reached my house, he escorted me halfway up the driveway, turned around, and quickly headed toward his car with a brief "Merry Christmas!" I say he actually ran; he says he merely "walked briskly." We both agree that he acted like a scared sixteen year old!

Two more months passed. The Israel trip came and went. Then one day in early February Elder Poelman called to see if I'd like to go out to dinner and the ballet. I accepted.

He continued, "I have a question. How do you feel about being seen with me in public?"

"I should think that would be of more concern to you than it is to me."

"It is!"

We both laughed. A rather long, remarkably comfortable conversation ensued. Our plans for the evening were complicated somewhat by my scheduled departure on an overnight flight to Florida for a vacation with my parents. But we eventually worked out all the details.

The designated evening finally arrived. After a quiet dinner at a restaurant near the theatre, we walked into the ballet. We immediately encountered what seemed like half of Salt Lake City in the lobby: several Relief Society board members, one of Ron's colleagues from the Seventy, two more of his brothers and their wives, and several colleagues of mine.

I don't remember much of the ballet. Neither does Ron. I was acutely aware of sitting next to him, our arms lightly touching. Afterward, we hastily departed for the airport. With only a bit more than ten minutes before the scheduled takeoff, Ron deposited me and my carry-on bag at the curb. "I really enjoyed the evening. It wasn't as bad as I thought," he confessed. I knew he didn't mean *me*; he was referring to the terrifying experience of dating for the first time after nearly thirty years of married life.

"I had a wonderful time too. Thank you."

"When you get back from Florida, perhaps we could get together again."

"I'd like that very much."

I disappeared into the airport and ran for the plane. I made it, but just barely. Later I wrote Ron a brief note from Florida, thanking him again for a lovely evening. I told my parents that I'd had an "interesting" date with a widower, but didn't elaborate.

I thought and prayed a great deal about my budding relationship—if a single date could be so called—with Ron. I certainly didn't love him; I scarcely knew him. But I sensed a certain inevitability about the relationship that frightened me more than a little.

I had also accepted an invitation from the Tampa, Florida, stake to fly in and speak at a special youth conference during my vacation. The stake president and his wife met me at the airport and took me to their home. After dinner the three of us settled in to get acquainted prior to the conference the following day.

"Anne, how are things going for you in Salt Lake City?" the

stake president inquired. I launched into an enthusiastic description of my professional activities but he stopped me mid-sentence. "No, that's not what I meant. How are things in your personal life?"

I was taken aback by the pointed question from someone I scarcely knew. Yet for some inexplicable reason, I felt completely comfortable in answering frankly. "It's sort of—interesting. I dated a great deal during the first few years after I moved to Salt Lake. Then I pretty much stopped dating. No one really appealed to me. Until recently. The night I left to come down here I had a date with a widower who is an attorney," I replied with deliberate vagueness.

"Is it Elder Poelman?" he inquired bluntly.

I was truly startled. "Yes. How did you know?"

"I just do. How do you feel about it?"

"Confused. A bit scared. I hardly know him."

"Would you like me to give you a priesthood blessing?" he asked kindly.

I had rarely requested such a blessing but readily accepted his thoughtful offer. I don't think I've ever had such a direct blessing, before or since. In the blessing the stake president told me that Elder Poelman would call and ask if he could pick me up at the airport in Salt Lake. He would then take me home and ask me to marry him, and I was supposed to say yes.

I felt an immediate calmness and knew that what he said would in fact happen. We all had tears in our eyes, knowing that together we had just experienced a direct message from the Lord.

After the youth conference the stake president and his wife returned me to the airport. When I promised to keep in touch, they laughingly declared, "Just invite us to the wedding!"

My parents met me at the West Palm Beach airport, a letter from Ron in hand. He wanted to pick me up in Salt Lake when I returned! Knowing then what would surely happen, I decided to prepare my parents for the event.

"Ron says in the letter that he wants to meet me at the airport when I fly back to Salt Lake City. I need to tell you something else. When he takes me home he'll ask me to marry him. And I'm going to say yes!"

My mother, obviously and understandably startled, asked, "Well, do you love him?"

My reply was honest but definite. "No. But I will."

I had my own "white knuckle" trip back to Salt Lake. The flight seemed interminable but we finally arrived. I walked up the jetway and could see Ron waiting in the concourse, smiling broadly. I gave him a brief hug—our first embrace—and we headed for the baggage claim area. He never said a word when my two suitcases and three big cardboard boxes tumbled down the chute. A good prognostic sign!

He took me home and I invited him in for a glass of fresh Florida orange juice. It was cold in the house; Ron readily accepted my invitation to build a fire in the fireplace and stay for a catch-up visit.

A huge fire blazing merrily away, we cautiously positioned ourselves at opposite ends of the sofa.

"You know," Ron said softly, "I've thought a lot about you while you were away."

"I've thought a lot about you too."

"I know we're both busy and your hospital schedule is often unpredictable. But I was really hoping perhaps we might spend some more time together. There're some things I need to say to you, but I'm not quite sure how to go about doing it."

I replied quietly, "That's not really necessary because I already know."

He looked me squarely in the eyes with unmitigated joy and relief. "Well, then!" he exclaimed. "Will you marry me?"

"Yes! What took you so long?"

We both laughed uproariously at the saucy exchange. And closed the distance on the couch.

Three months later, Ron and I were sealed together in the Salt Lake Temple. We've been married for nearly thirteen wonderful years. Improbable as our courtship and marriage seems, it really happened like that. In retrospect, I think it's a classic example of the Simeon Solution at work: Be obedient, stay faithful, trust in the Lord. Be patient and remain spiritually centered. Stand firm in the faith.

Of course I can't promise every single brother or sister in the Church such a dramatic result. But I do firmly believe that our Heavenly Father is in charge, and that's sufficient. The Lord knows each one of us individually, personally, and intimately. He knows our innermost yearnings. He hears the earnest, prayerful pleadings of our hearts. He has promised that if we strive to live righteously and keep his commandments, he will pour out uncounted blessings on us. But the timing and specific nature of those blessings is up to him.

There's a bit of the miraculous in most people's lives, however mundane those lives may seem to them. For example, ask a convert how he or she came to join the Church, and watch for an interesting response. Or ask a happily married couple how they met. The latter is no mere conversational gambit, although it's usually a successful one. Try it sometime. Watch people's faces as they smile in wonder and recognition at the Lord's guidance of those long-ago events. Truly, if we're patient, faithful, and open to promptings from the Spirit, the Lord can and does work joyous miracles in our lives.

Chapter 15

Adversity

A storybook romance, a blissfully happy married life, a productive career doing worthwhile things, and meaningful Church service. It couldn't last forever, could it?

Certainly not. And it didn't.

Late summer of that fateful year had already been a particularly stressful time for both Ron and me, filled with demanding work and pressing family concerns. The transient rest and relaxation we had enjoyed during a brief July break was replaced with August's relentless schedule.

The General Authorities' common occupational hazard, fatigue, was etched on Ron's face as he sat down to eat a hurried breakfast one Saturday morning before heading to the airport.

"Sweetheart, you look really tired," I remarked with concern, putting a bowl of freshly picked raspberries in front of him.

"I'm really beat," he admitted. "I haven't been sleeping well. Lots on my mind. And there never seems to be enough time to get everything that needs to be done . . .

I was startled to see he had fallen sound asleep mid-sentence. The poor guy was so exhausted he couldn't even stay awake to eat breakfast! *Let him sleep,* I decided.

Half an hour passed while I quietly cleaned up the kitchen,

trying not to disturb him. Ron was immobile, out cold. But time was finally getting tight, and I didn't want him to miss his plane. I whispered in his ear, "Ron, time to wake up."

No response.

I kissed him on the cheek. "Sweetheart, we need to get going."

Still no response.

I gently but insistently shook his arm. "Ron, please wake up! Time to go!"

He opened his eyes. Looking confused and disoriented, he silently stared at the bowl of raspberries. He shook his head, trying vainly to clear his mind, then slowly reached for the spoon.

And missed!

I watched with mounting horror as he tried again, clumsily grasping the spoon in his fist. I felt frozen in stunned disbelief as he spilled the berries down his bathrobe.

This isn't happening! my mind screamed in frightened protest. But it was.

"Ron, I . . . "

He looked at me blankly, then tried to talk. His speech was slurred and thick.

This is a bad dream. A nightmare, I told myself again. *It isn't real. Strokes happen to other people. Patients. Not my husband!*

I struggled to compose myself, the doctor-half of me dispassionately making the diagnosis and already planning for the medical emergency while the wife-half was still immobilized from sheer terror.

The doctor-half won, at least temporarily. "Ron," I said decisively, "you're having a stroke. We need to get you to the hospital. Right now."

"No, I'm okay." His speech was better but still thick.

Not wanting to argue and risk upsetting him, I temporarily

compromised. "All right. Just lie down on the couch in the living room so I can check your blood pressure." I helped him into the living room, noting his poor balance and his staggering, hesitant gait.

He stretched out obediently while I took his blood pressure. It was elevated—not critically, but high enough to be worrisome.

"I'm feeling better now," he said. "I need to get dressed." His speech was improving by the minute, to my vast relief. It still wasn't normal but it was definitely better.

"Sweetheart," I replied, "you've had a stroke. We need to get to the hospital."

"No," he insisted. "I need to go right to the airport. I can't miss my conference."

"Well, let's get you dressed first. Then we can decide whether we drive to the hospital or the airport." I knew which it would have to be, but I didn't want to make him anxious and further raise his already high blood pressure.

I helped him up the stairs, then sat and watched as he valiantly tried to dress. He couldn't get his leg into his pants. He clenched his jaw as he kept trying and missing. Frustrated, he finally looked up and reluctantly conceded, "Something really is wrong with me. My legs won't work right. My coordination is off. Let's go to the hospital."

I quickly called the emergency room at University Hospital, asked them to alert the neurology resident and on-call attending faculty, and drove Ron up the hill. The E.R. team was waiting as we sped into the portico. Gently but quickly they transferred Ron to a waiting wheeled cart and pushed him into an empty treatment room.

Knowing that his care was now in the capable hands of the E.R. team and the senior staff neurologists, I collapsed into a chair and wept. The cool, controlled doctor persona evaporated. All that was left was Worried Wife.

Each snippet of good news, no matter how small, seemed supremely important. I grasped desperately at each medical life preserver tossed into my own raging sea of emotional turmoil.

Ron's symptoms, at least the worst of them, continued to improve slowly. The CAT scan showed no bleeding into the brain. Good news. The angiogram, an imaging study that depicts the brain's blood vessels, showed an abnormally enlarged main artery where the flow slowed, tending to form clots that could break off and plug branches that supplied blood to critical areas of the brain. Bad news.

The diagnostic and laboratory studies completed, Ron was wheeled into a spacious, quiet room on the neurosciences floor. I sat by his bedside, hypnotized by the slow drip-drip-drip of life-saving blood thinners from the intravenous infusion suspended overhead. The whole situation seemed completely surreal.

A steady stream of residents and attending doctors came and went. They examined Ron, poking and prodding, tapping his knees and elbows with ubiquitous rubber hammers, pricking his skin, making him walk and talk and count fingers. *Perform like some poor circus animal,* I thought.

I seemed invisible as the doctors conferred with each other in hushed tones. "Unusual clinical presentation," I heard the senior neurologist say to a group of attentive medical students and interns. "Probably a small embolus to one of the pontine perforating branches off that ectatic basilar artery. Temporarily knocked out the RAS."

Medical gobbledygook. On the receiving end for a change, I irrationally thought they all talked like that so patients and their families wouldn't know what they were saying. You know, like

116

speaking a foreign language right in front of others who of course can't understand. Rude, isn't it? Down deep inside I really knew better; medicalese was a spare, technical language that described precisely what was being observed. But seen from the other side it seemed cruelly opaque and impersonal.

"Interesting case," the senior resident commented.

Interesting case! My husband? I thought, outraged.

His demeanor shifting from professor to concerned colleague, the senior neurologist turned to me and explained, "Ron's had a posterior fossa transient ischemic attack." That was medicalese for a "warning stroke" in the back of the brain.

He continued, "Fortunately, most of the symptoms have cleared. He has a bit of residual dysarthria and ataxia but I think that will eventually resolve, too." The speech and walking problems would get better. Good news.

"However . . ."

The catch. There always seems to be a "however."

"The angiogram showed rather severe vertebrobasilar dolichoectasia with very sluggish blood flow. I think Ron's superb cardiovascular conditioning probably saved his life. He was somehow able to maintain some posterior fossa perfusion until the clot lysed. So he had ischemia rather than frank infarction. He has recovered remarkably well. But he'll be at risk for the rest of his life. I would recommend gradually weaning him off the heparin drip and onto oral anticoagulants."

That was sobering news. It meant that unless Ron's blood could be "thinned" successfully, the abnormal blood vessel would continue to be a source of problems. This time he had escaped with virtually no brain damage. The next time he might not be so lucky.

"What happens if he's anticoagulated and he falls and hits his head? Or has another stroke and this time it bleeds?" I asked, already knowing the likely answer.

"That's the risk, of course, but I don't really see much in the way of alternatives," the neurologist answered. "It's not a surgically amenable lesion. Medical therapy is the only realistic treatment."

I sighed despondently, knowing the knife-edge balance Ron would walk for the rest of his life, however long and precarious that might be. The neurologist patted my shoulder sympathetically, gathered his team together, and left to see other patients.

Ron's brothers had been standing outside the room, patiently waiting until the doctors completed their rounds. They all filed in, hugged me, and surrounded the bed. Everyone had the sense not to make halfhearted jokes in an attempt to alleviate the somber mood. After solicitous inquiries and expressions of love and support, they gave him a priesthood blessing. It was full of hope and comfort.

We all felt better.

Not wanting to tire Ron, his brothers left after the brief visit and I was momentarily alone with him. "Sweetheart," I said, finally needing to break the tension, "if you die and leave me with all that new exercise equipment at home, I'm going to be mad as all heck!"

Ron grinned weakly, "I'll do my best. I have no intention of leaving you. With or without the equipment!" He closed his eyes, exhausted with the effort of speaking, and was soon sound asleep.

Needing time and space to reflect, I slipped out of the room and went down to my office—a quiet place on a Saturday afternoon. Sinking into a chair, I buried my face in my hands. The merciful numbness of the immediate shock was wearing off as awful reality came crashing in.

There was a soft knock on the door. I opened it reluctantly. Lucy, my pediatrician sister, walked in, steadying herself with her cane. She hugged me, saying, "I thought I might find you here."

We both sat down.

"Ron was sleeping when I dropped by. The neurologist says most of the neurologic deficit has cleared. He's going to be okay." Lucy paused, then perceptively asked, "So how are *you* doing, Annie?"

"I'm not sure," I confessed. "It all happened so unexpectedly. I guess what's hardest now is that all of a sudden life seems so uncertain."

"Annie, it always was. You just didn't recognize it," she said with a wry smile. Lucy has multiple sclerosis, the chronic relapsing-remitting kind, and wakes up each morning facing the distinct possibility that another part of her body won't work right.

I nodded at her insight, reluctantly acknowledging this unwanted intrusion of new anxieties into my life. After a few additional comments and another hug thrown in for good measure, we walked together toward the hospital's main entrance. It was a surprisingly beautiful day. Tired of trying to cope with everything, I decided to take a brief walk.

Everyone seemed so normal. People sat on benches, chatting happily and munching on sandwiches, oblivious to the awful event that had just transpired. How could they? Why weren't they grief stricken, as I was?

The sun was blindingly brilliant. Why hadn't it stopped in its tracks, acknowledging the sudden event that had wrenched our lives irretrievably out of mold?

Orderlies and technicians on break were playing basketball. The *thunk-thunk* of a dribble and then the *clank* of a missed shot ricocheting off the iron rim annoyed me. Why weren't they standing still, in silent respect and prayer for Ron's life? *They don't even realize,* I thought.

Everything seemed so normal, and yet I knew it wasn't and never would be, ever again. The ebb and flow of daily life continued unabated; the humdrum activities swirled all around and left me feeling isolated, fearful, and resentful.

When I returned to Ron's room, it was filled with flowers and fruit baskets, cards and helium-filled balloons. The first of many General Authority visitors had already arrived. As they came and went I found myself envying their robust good health, resenting their cheerful demeanor and unfailing optimism.

"Don't worry about your assignments," they said to Ron, "they're covered. Take as much time as you need," they added.

Baloney, I thought in wounded suspicion. *What you really mean is, how much time will you miss? When can you get back? Are you going to be fully functional?* I knew it wasn't rational, but I enjoyed the brief surge of righteous indignation I felt. It was better than feeling so alone and vulnerable.

Sunday evening, Elders Dean Larsen, then the Senior President of the Seventy, and Burke Peterson, with whom Ron was serving in the Southwest Area Presidency, returned to Salt Lake City from their own weekend assignments. At Ron's request, they had been the first ones notified of his condition.

When they walked into the room, I quickly put on my now-practiced mask of professional detachment and controlled wifely concern. The two men grasped Ron's arms in warm greeting, then turned to me and asked, "How's he doing?"

Standard question. Funny how people often talk about the sick individual in the third person. I gave the standard answer, reciting the event and the guarded but hopeful prognosis in a tired litany.

They both paused, then gently guided me into the hallway, out of earshot. "And how are *you* doing?"

The dam finally broke. Long-suppressed tears welled up and all the grief and anxiety spilled out in a flood. I was angry with the Lord for letting it happen to us. I resented the Church because of the relentless schedule I was sure had contributed to Ron's stroke. I was sad. I was mad. I was confused. I wasn't sure *what* I felt.

To their great credit and my eternal gratitude, those two good brethren didn't protest. They didn't offer false assurances. They didn't even offer a mild but justifiable rebuke, "Oh, you mustn't feel that way."

They just let me talk. They understood. And when I had finally finished running the gamut of my emotions, they gave me my own special blessing.

I'm not sure who was healed more, Ron or me. He did recover. In fact, only careful examination by an expert neurologist would disclose even minor residual problems. He does have to be very careful, but perhaps that's good.

Both of us learned some important things from that experience. We no longer take health and well-being for granted. We recognize life for the great blessing it is. It's true that I don't know what challenges tomorrow might bring. Frankly, I try not to think about it too much. But I do know one thing: whatever happens, it'll be okay. I waited a long time for Ron; I could do it again, if necessary. It would be hard, but with an eternal perspective and trust in the Lord, all things are possible. And bearable, too.

Chapter 16

Unity or Uniformity?

The annual North America Central Area Mission Presidents' Seminar was approaching rapidly. This particular year the meeting was to be held under the direction of Elder Neal A. Maxwell. At the time, Ron was serving in the Area Presidency and we were consequently both invited to attend the seminar in historic Nauvoo, Illinois.

Mission presidents' seminars, traditionally three-day events that include instructional, spiritual, and some recreational activities, are carefully planned and greatly anticipated by the leaders and their wives. Much prayerful, thoughtful consideration is given to both the content and structure of these important meetings.

All the participants, namely the General Authorities and their wives as well as the mission presidents and their wives, would attend plenary sessions of this conference. A special breakout session for the wives had also been included in the packed schedule. As wife of the presiding senior Apostle, Sister Colleen Maxwell was our designated leader. She was acutely conscious of her responsibilities as well as very much aware of the unique nature of our special meeting and the opportunities it presented.

Well in advance of the meeting, Sister Maxwell asked the other General Authorities' wives to meet with her and discuss ideas about the session. Several suggestions were offered that might maximize the meeting's effectiveness. As is nearly always the case, the number of potential discussion items far outweighed the relatively limited time allowed for them.

After hearing everyone out, Sister Maxwell began to assign responsibilities. I, the youngest and by far the least experienced member of the group, was greatly relieved when the program was nearly complete and my name hadn't been mentioned.

My relief didn't last.

"Annie," Sister Maxwell said, turning to me, "I think we should hear from you at the meeting."

I groaned inwardly but still hoped my participation might be a relatively simple assignment, something like giving the closing prayer.

No such luck. "In fact," she added, "the more I think about it, the more I feel you should lead the discussion period. You could take a few minutes at the beginning and then open the discussion up to everyone."

Oh, no! I thought. I had only attended two other mission presidents' seminars and knew that such an assignment required the wisdom of experience combined with a real feeling for the challenges the sisters faced on a daily basis.

"Colleen," I demurred, "you know I'll do whatever you ask. But I feel really strange about the whole thing. I'm a convert. I didn't grow up in the Church. I've never been on a mission. I've never had children. I know zip about teenagers. And I've never cooked for the masses, either! What in the world would I talk about? What could I say that anyone doesn't already know better than I do?"

Everyone chuckled at my obvious discomfort.

Sister Maxwell was insistent. "Annie, we're putting you on the program for the discussion."

Later I spoke to her privately. "Are you sure about this?" I inquired dubiously.

She smiled, "I'm sure."

"What do you think we should discuss?"

"Frankly, I don't know."

"*You don't know!*" my panic rose a notch.

"No. But you will," she said gently but firmly.

I've never lost any sleep over giving medical lectures or delivering a scientific paper to an audience of thousands. But I experienced a lot of wakeful nights after Sister Maxwell's assignment. I prayed about it intensely and knew she was right. I was supposed to speak briefly and then lead the main discussion. On what topic, I hadn't the faintest idea.

I prayed about the specific subject and got no answer. There would be plenty of doctrinal discussions in the plenary sessions, and I didn't think more of the same would be appropriate.

Desperate for suggestions, I called several women I knew who had been mission presidents' wives. Some had interesting ideas but they just didn't seem quite right for us. I even thought of calling half a dozen women who were "old hands" and asking each one for her best two or three recipes to serve a minimum of twenty!

With barely a week left before the seminar, I had almost concluded this would have to be one of those times when "it shall be given you in that same hour what ye shall speak" (Matthew 10:19).

Then, quite suddenly and unexpectedly, the answer came.

The Midwest in late autumn is glorious. The suffocating heat and high humidity of summer have faded, yielding to pleasantly

124

sunny days and cool, crisp evenings. Silos and corn cribs are filled to bursting with the rich harvest and the fertile, loamy fields are meticulously plowed and fertilized in anticipation of the next plantings. Produce stands spring up along country roads, offering pumpkins, Indian corn, assorted decorative gourds, late-harvest pears, and homemade jams. The fall colors are past their peak, but a few leaves cling tenaciously to barren branches and brightly colored berries accent the dense underbrush.

We drove across the broad, lazy Mississippi River toward the Nauvoo lowlands. After freshening up at our hotel, we had a lovely dinner and retired early in anticipation of the next day's crowded schedule.

Ron and I arose before dawn to jog through the restored town and around the old temple site, then turned down along the river bank. The air was pungent, redolent with earthy odors and the damp smell of the nearby Mississippi. I would have enjoyed the spectacular dawn had I not felt so nervous. Mercifully, I didn't have an interminably long wait. The sisters' seminar was scheduled for the afternoon session of the first day.

The opening session was truly outstanding. Elder Maxwell presided and welcomed everyone. After the introductions he spoke briefly, then called on several members of the Area Presidencies (including Ron) to speak. Elder Maxwell then filled the balance of the morning with an extraordinarily inspiring talk about Joseph Smith. We sat spellbound as he expressed his deep love for Joseph Smith and delineated some of the Prophet's most profound doctrinal insights. Engrossed in the ideas Elder Maxwell was discussing so movingly, I temporarily forgot my nervous apprehension.

Lunch was over in a flash and the sisters started gathering for our breakout meeting. They were excited and upbeat as they chatted together prior to the afternoon session. I said little, wondering if what I had planned would really work.

The wives relaxed visibly as Sister Maxwell started the meeting, immediately putting everyone at ease with her gracious manner and approachable personality. A promising beginning.

After the opening hymn and prayer, Sister Maxwell and the wives of the other two Area Presidency members spoke. She then announced that the balance of the afternoon would be an open, informal discussion that she had asked me to lead after I made some brief introductory remarks. She told them a bit about me, then sat down.

I stood up, praying silently, *Lord, please let it work.*

"Sisters," I said, unable to keep the nervous tension from my voice, "when Sister Maxwell gave me this assignment, I had no idea what to do. I feel really inadequate. Who am I to be teaching you? You've all been members of the Church longer than I have. You know the scriptures and the doctrines. You've already been out in the mission field for periods varying from a few months to over two years. I've never even been on a mission myself."

I could see a few wordless protests forming. "No," I continued, "I have little experience as a General Authority's wife. Ron and I have been married for just six years. I've never had children. In fact, Ron tells me my theories of child-raising—based purely on abstract ideas and not one whit in practical experience—would curl your hair!"

They laughed and I felt better.

"I don't know beans about teenagers. I've never cooked for more than a dozen people in my life. What I'm really good at is diagnosing brain tumors and strokes, and I hope that will never be very useful for you. So I really pondered and prayed about what the Lord wanted us to discuss this afternoon. It took some time, but I feel I finally received the answer. I'd like to talk with you about discouragement, depression, and their malignant cousin, despair."

I could hear a sharp intake of breath as the sisters reacted to this unexpected turn. I continued, "We all feel discouraged from time to time. Such feelings are normal when our responsibilities seem overwhelming and unremitting. Personal resources are strained and feelings of inadequacy are exacerbated when the demands and expectations of others exceed our ability to meet them.

"Frankly, at first I felt really discouraged when Sister Maxwell gave me this assignment. I couldn't imagine what I could ever bring to this discussion that might be helpful. I thought and prayed about it. For a long time I didn't have the slightest clue. It made me feel inadequate, even a bit desperate. Maybe that's part of the process: learning to recognize our own shortcomings. Realizing our dependence on the Lord and somehow learning to cope with always falling short is another part."

I talked about the difference between feeling discouraged and being depressed. I then asked the sisters what they thought depression really was. How could it be recognized and helped? Did they know anyone who might be suffering from depression?

At first the sisters hesitated, each reluctant to be the first to comment. When one finally spoke up, the dam broke.

The afternoon flew by. When Ron opened the door to gather us for the closing session, the sisters were still talking animatedly. Realistically. Hopefully. Helpfully. And about a topic they had initially felt reluctant to discuss.

Those sisters felt good. I did too. My inexperience and different background hadn't been a handicap at all. In fact, it was okay, and safe, to express openly our feelings of inadequacy. To me that's one of the most wonderful things about the Church. Years later, I occasionally encounter some of those sisters. They still talk about that unusual session and how helpful it was in dealing with some of their missionaries.

That experience helped me recognize that each of us has a special, even unique role to serve in the kingdom. Uniformity is not necessary or even desirable; unity is. My life circumstances were very different from those of the mission presidents' and other General Authorities' wives. Yet our testimonies, firm commitment to the gospel, and dedication to the Lord's church united us.

The Apostle Paul stated, "Ye are all one in Christ Jesus" (Galatians 3:28). The Savior himself prayed to the Father that his apostles and all the saints "may be one, as we are" (John 17:11). The unity of which Jesus spoke does not require us to become identical. It does entreat us as individuals to be of one mind and purpose in our shared commitment to the kingdom.

Chapter 17

Growing a Testimony

Its diesel engine finally stilled, the old but sturdy fishing boat rose and fell passively on the broad, deep Caribbean swells. The silence was punctuated by the sharp, rhythmic slap of waves against the weathered hull. A seagull hovered hopefully overhead and cried plaintively, attempting to coax a handout from the crew.

The hot sun beat down in a cloudless, brassy sky as Ron and I peered somewhat apprehensively over the side into the brilliant blue water. Far below, the sandy, shell-strewn bottom looked deceptively close.

It was over fifty feet down.

The ocean floor sloped gently toward a spectacular coral reef that curved away into the distance, paralleling the beach that was by now barely visible on the horizon. Just beyond its crest, the reef below us abruptly disappeared in a vertical ledge that overhung a seemingly bottomless trench. The depths past the protective reef yawned in an inky, toothless grin.

I shivered involuntarily despite the scorching heat. Suddenly our much-anticipated "second honeymoon" assumed an ominous air. Perhaps Ron and I should have remained safely on the beach with the other sunscreen-coated tourists, sipping fresh guava juice under the tall coconut palms that rustled invitingly in the hot, humid air. And doing completely innocuous things like reading historical novels and napping in the shade.

Maybe we really were too old for this scuba diving stuff. It had seemed like such an adventuresome idea at the time. Intriguing signs posted on the wall of the hotel's beach shack invited tourists to sign up for lessons; we had yielded to the allure of the tempting underwater photos depicting brilliantly colored fish and exotic coral formations.

We started with the usual landlubber classes and required reading assignments. Our first actual experience with diving itself was within the safe but sterile confines of the hotel's large pool. We were taught how to don snorkeling gear properly and clear the water from our face masks. Once we became adept at those basic techniques, we were allowed to put on leaded weight belts, buoyancy compensator vests, and finally the heavy tanks of compressed air with their hoses and regulators.

It was fun. It was exhilarating. Freed from the mammalian necessity of periodically coming up for air, we paddled around in the pool's deep end, happily gesturing at each other and exhaling bubbles that spiraled in lazy circles toward the mirrored surface. Except for the pale bodies of vacationing swimmers occasionally splashing through the surface above us, the pool was devoid of activity. We soon became bored with its monotony and longed for our first real dive.

It wasn't long in coming. The next day our instructor took us for our first open-water excursion, a shallow dive in the island's nearby harbor. We dived down to the decaying hulk of an old boat that had sunk in about twenty feet of water. It would be romantic to say it was a long lost Spanish galleon bound for exotic ports with its cargo of purloined New World treasure, but in reality it was an old, dilapidated, World War II era tugboat. It didn't matter. We thought it was wonderfully exciting anyway.

But today's dive was qualitatively different. We had quickly left the calm harbor as the boat headed through the sheltering breakwaters, then turned and chugged steadily toward the open sea. After motoring for nearly an hour, the captain reached the designated spot and the dive guide quickly let out the anchor. The heavy, rusted chain seemed to unreel forever before the anchor hooked firmly into the sea bottom.

Ron and I were both uneasy about the deepwater dive. I secretly wanted to call the whole thing off but didn't want to disappoint him. He later told me he had felt like bowing out himself but didn't want to ruin the dive for me. So we were both stuck, reluctant partners in a suddenly and quite unexpectedly intimidating adventure.

Ron flopped awkwardly across the deck in his swim fins as the dive guide helped him into his weight belt and strapped the unwieldy tank of compressed air to his back. "Hey, no problem, mon," he assured Ron.

Ron grinned crookedly, unconvinced.

The guide slipped easily into his own gear, then sat on the boat's gunwale and explained to Ron how simple it really was. You just put the regulator in your mouth, held your mask firmly with one hand, and tumbled over the side backwards into the water. He demonstrated by leaning back and disappearing with a loud splash.

Ron looked at me and winked encouragingly. "No problem, mon," he mimicked. He shoved the regulator in his mouth, exhaled forcefully through it to blow any retained water out of the valves, took a couple of deep whooshing breaths from the tank, and was gone.

My turn. The captain looked at me questioningly, raising his eyebrows. I nodded resignedly and put on the gear.

Balancing on the gunwale of the pitching craft was harder than it looked. The boat lurched just as I was readying the regulator's mouthpiece. I abruptly lost my equilibrium and with a dismayed squawk fell overboard prematurely.

The shock of the cool water and my unexpected twisting somersault temporarily disoriented me. I couldn't tell which direction was up. The face mask filled with salty water, stinging my eyes and blurring my vision. I felt a sudden surge of panic until I remembered the lifesaving air that was strapped securely on my back. I fumbled for the hose and quickly found the regulator. Clearing it with a blast of air from the tank, I clamped my teeth on the mouthpiece, blew out the residual water, and inhaled deeply. Rubber-tainted air filled my lungs.

After a few rapid, greedy gasps, my breathing gradually slowed to nearly normal. No problem, mon! The gear worked fine, just as it had in the pool. Reassured about the independent air supply, I cleared the mask as we had been taught. All of a sudden everything came into sharp, clear focus. I was surrounded by a school of gaudily colored, variegated tropical fish. I could see the hull of the boat above, rocking gently with the waves as it tugged on the anchor chain. Fifty feet below, Ron and the guide were hovering near the bottom, gesticulating encouragingly for me to come on down.

No problem, mon, I thought again and let some air out of the buoyancy vest, beginning the slow-motion descent.

A sharp, growing pain in my eardrums interrupted the pleasant reverie. I had forgotten to equalize pressure between my middle ear and nasopharynx. I closed my mouth, held my nose, and forced air out. Both ears abruptly popped and to my relief the pain promptly disappeared.

Suspended weightlessly in the blue depths, fears forgotten, I eased into a deliciously slow somersault as I sank toward the bottom, luxuriating in the unbelievably liberating experience of complete freedom from gravity.

A soft, gentle stirring of fine white sand heralded my arrival on the ocean floor. I gave Ron and the guide the thumbs-up sign that meant "okay—all is well." The guide gestured for us to follow him as he slowly swam toward the reef looming in the blue-green distance.

I'll never forget our first close-up glimpse of that majestic coral reef. From the surface it had appeared relatively small and insignificant, somewhat resembling a miniature replica in a pet store fish tank. But from the perspective of the ocean floor, the reef was huge. It towered upwards for twenty or thirty feet and stretched in both directions until it disappeared out of sight in the hazy distance.

The reef was truly magnificent. It literally teemed with life. Fish of every size and hue darted in and out of innumerable hiding places. The reef's coral infrastructure was itself a dynamic, living thing, deposited millimeter by millimeter by an incredible variety of microorganisms. Over the centuries some had formed treelike excrescences that projected at odd angles from the main ridge line itself. Others formed rounded knobs or graceful, corrugated fans that decorated the outcroppings along the bank.

The reef was host to a veritable seaquarium of wildlife that lived in its nooks and crannies. Tiny tube worms peeked out of delicately elongated coral straws, their colorful feather-duster feelers swaying in the undersea currents until, somehow warned of our approach by a subtle change in water pressure, they abruptly disappeared inside their hollow cones.

Sea urchins nestled in rounded-out crevices along the reef, their surfaces gaily festooned with small shells and rocks. Spiny, misshapen fish that had evolved defensive coloration nearly identical to the reef itself were scarcely perceptible as they hid in its protective embrace. Moray eels eyed us suspiciously from their dark caves as we swam by. Even a few sharp-toothed, cigar-shaped barracuda slowly cruised the reef, looking for easy prey.

Thank goodness there were no sharks.

Time literally flew by as we swam with fish that circled around us, curious but unafraid. I was astonished at their variety and their rich, nearly fluorescent coloring. As if directed by some unseen choreographer, the schools slowly wheeled and turned in shimmering, flashing curtains of color. We even saw a baby octopus that briefly waved its tentacles at us before scuttling away to hide shyly beneath the reef.

The dive guide, intimately familiar with the reef's geography and population, pointed out a gigantic lobster that clacked and snapped its claws at us menacingly. Our guide left it alone for future undersea tourists to enjoy.

The coral reef and its denizens were a whole new universe, one we'd never imagined could be so completely engrossing. It was beautiful. It was wonderful. It was magic.

All too soon the dive was over. As we had been taught, we periodically checked the gauges on our tanks. We had started with a full air supply, nearly 3000 pounds per square inch. My indicator had been dropping steadily and was now hovering around 750 p.s.i.; 500 p.s.i. was the designated minimum with which to begin the gradual ascent toward the surface.

I looked around for the familiar anchor chain. It was nowhere in sight and I hadn't the faintest clue in which direction it was. To my relief the dive guide swam up and gestured toward the surface, beckoning us to follow him. He finned off vigorously into the distance as we tagged along behind his rapidly disappearing silhouette.

It seemed like we swam forever, but eventually we could see the waiting boat above us, rocking rhythmically. Holding onto the anchor chain, we slowly ascended toward the surface, periodically pausing to adjust for the lessening water pressure.

In sharp contrast to the tranquil depths below, the currents just under the wind-roughened waves were stiff and turbulent. As I popped through the glittering surface into the warm, buttery sunlight above, I kept the regulator safely in my mouth and inflated the buoyancy vest fully. I bobbed in the waves and clung precariously to the anchor chain as the guide boosted Ron onto the platform that jutted off the boat's stern. He unbuckled his gear and the captain hauled the cumbersome tank and backpack over the side into the boat. Then Ron climbed in and gratefully wrapped himself in a warm, dry towel, politely but firmly declining the readily proffered cup of raw Jamaican rum.

I followed the same routine. Despite the blazing hot sun, I found myself shivering uncontrollably—not out of fear but from mild hypothermia. Spending forty-five minutes submerged in seventy-six-degree water without a wetsuit does that. My skin looked pale and bleached, shriveled from the prolonged saltwater immersion.

Legs trembling a bit from the exertion, Ron and I looked at each other and grinned exultantly. We had done it! We felt exhausted but happy and fulfilled.

The underwater environment was completely unlike anything we had ever experienced before. To function safely and successfully in such unfamiliar surroundings, we had to relearn a very familiar set of principles and then applied them to a new situation:

1. Focus on the fundamental principles of safety. Rules are there for a reason. Ignoring or flouting them could have unpleasant—even fatal—consequences.
2. Seek out an experienced instructor. A certified one. Don't depend on the advice of amateurs or self-styled experts.
3. Practice and prepare in a safe, predictable environment before exploring unfamiliar territory.
4. Follow the guide's directions with exactness! After all, he's been there before.
5. Don't go off exploring alone. The "buddy system" really works!
6. Closely monitor where you are and what your resources are (in this case, air). Keep careful track of your "buddy," too. So-called "rapture of the deep" (underwater euphoria and mental dysfunction induced by overextending a dive) is a dangerous, real phenomenon.

In all areas of life, spiritual as well as physical, carefully obeying those simple fundamentals results in genuine freedom, freedom to explore safely and enjoy the discovery of an exciting new realm.

Furthermore, as Ron and I have reflected on our scuba diving experience, I've realized that in many respects my testimony of the gospel grew much like that coral reef must have done.

Once upon a time, there was no reef at all where we took our first deep dive. Perhaps propelled by unseen underwater currents, sediment began to accumulate gradually and the first few micro-organisms found homes in the promising spot. Those tiny inhabitants multiplied and attracted more. Other species gathered and made their home in the nascent reef. Day after day, year after year, a millimeter at a time, the reef grew. With the passage of decades and perhaps even centuries, those first few humble coral clumps became an imposing, breathtaking, living edifice.

It's only in retrospect that the slow, steady deposition of a coral reef can be appreciated. The actual day-to-day changes pass completely unnoticed, even by an acute observer.

For me, coming to realize that the Church really is true was very similar. That knowledge was born of a thousand small but uplifting, edifying experiences. It was nurtured by prayerful, serious gospel study as I pondered the scriptures and read the inspired teachings of the Lord's anointed prophets. It grew through service to others. It was proven over and over by the practical, day-to-day "experiments" of which the prophet Alma spoke so eloquently. The indisputable evidence accumulated bit by bit, little by little.

Persistence pays off. The Lord has counseled us clearly on that point: "Wherefore, be not weary in well-doing, for ye are laying the foundation of a great work. *And out of small things proceedeth that which is great*" (D&C 64:33; italics added).

For many, if not most of us, a testimony is built, not bestowed. "Growing" a testimony takes both time and patience. It requires experience and service, hard work and determination.

With effort and experience, I found the gospel truly nourished my soul and literally became "delicious" to me. Friends, family, and even colleagues commented on its gentling, tempering effect on my life and personal relationships. I became a better person although by no means a perfect one.

As with observing the coral reef, it's only in retrospect that I can appreciate and identify the growth of my firm knowledge that the Church is indeed true. That testimony also developed with the passage of time and accumulated experience. Its growth was satisfyingly rapid at some times, agonizingly slow and almost imperceptible at others.

There were even a few occasions when it seemed as though my spiritual progress was actually reversed. I discovered that frustration arising from personal disappointments, troubling encounters, or unresolved doctrinal issues could gnaw at the foundations of my belief.

By trial—and sometimes error, too—I gradually learned to cope with unsettling circumstances by examining them in the context of my whole belief and experience. I look at things this way: The Lord has guided my life in the past, so I need to be patient and trust him. After all, he is still in charge. The Church is true, so I don't need to have neat answers to all my questions. I need to relax and put them on that old spiritual "back burner" for a season. That's the real essence of the Simeon Solution.

I'm convinced that, just as the foundation of our testimonies grows by accretion from many small and simple things, so it can be eroded gradually by the corrosive acid of discontent. Faith is rarely destroyed in some single, cataclysmic spiritual catastrophe. More often its loss is like picking up a handful of the fine, siltlike sand that lies on the ocean floor and feeling it gradually slip through your grasp grain by grain. Then it's gone.

We need to watch warily for the small and simple faith destroyers. A gripe here. A real or perceived slight there. A little doctrinal burr under the saddle. The microscopic slivers of discontent that, if left unattended, can incite a festering abscess that will poison our very soul.

The best antidotes for those difficult situations are trust, patience, and positive experiences. Service is a big boon; as we take care of others, the Lord will take care of our needs and concerns. He's done so in the past. He'll do so in the future.

Like the coral reef, the last important principle of the "Simeon Solution" evolved over a long time. When I was investigating the Church it began simply with the impression that I was on the track of something infinitely precious and worthwhile. As I tested gospel principles by believing without knowing, by acting on faith, the Spirit taught me through experiences the last, great, summarizing principle of the Simeon Solution, the one that is interwoven inextricably with all the others:

8. I know the Church is true.

Chapter 18

Horse Sense

The General Authorities' traditional July break is a much needed time for rest and recuperation. No stake or regional conferences are scheduled during the month and the relentless meeting schedule temporarily subsides.

Ron and I usually take the opportunity to escape Salt Lake City's summer heat for a few days. Several years ago we decided to visit Santa Fe, New Mexico. I had seen an appealing ad in *Sunset* magazine that touted the pleasant days, cool evenings, and multicultural charm of the old territorial capital. We tried it, liked it, and have been going there ever since.

Our favorite spot is the Bishop's Lodge, a quiet, rustic place nestled in Tesuque Canyon at the foot of the Sangre de Cristo mountains. The Bishop's Lodge is famed as the site of Willa Cather's *Death Comes for the Archbishop*.

There's no longer a bishop at the Bishop's Lodge. But they do have horses. Lots of them. I grew up with horses and love to ride. The first time we stayed at the Lodge, I noticed an attractively illustrated poster near the registration desk advertising "Breakfast Rides."

"Ron, look! They have horses!"

He grimaced.

I ignored his dubious look. "See, it says here, 'For riders of all experience levels, novice to expert.'"

"I've never reached a satisfactory accommodation with a horse," he said.

Hoping to convince him by appealing to his stomach, I rambled on. "It also says, 'Genuine Western chuck-wagon breakfast.'"

Ron's a good sport. "Well, I'm willing to give it a try," he conceded gracefully.

We signed up. As requested, we listed age, weight, and riding experience. I put down "experienced." Peeking over Ron's shoulder, I watched him write, "Never been on a horse before."

I protested. "That's not true. You told me you've been riding once or twice before!"

"Only after a fashion," he replied. "When I was nine or ten years old, we visited some relatives who lived on a farm in southern Utah. While the adults were talking, I went exploring. I saw a horse standing inside the corral with a saddle on its back. So I sneaked up, walking along the fence until I was just above it. Then I jumped into the saddle. The next thing I remember was waking up, lying in bed with a beefsteak on my eyes!"

I was horrified.

"You can guess what had happened," he continued. "The horse was a two-year-old colt they were just starting to break. My uncle had put the saddle on the horse's back so he'd get used to it before someone actually rode him for the first time. He'd never been ridden before. So when I innocently jumped into the saddle he bucked me off in a split second, and I hit my head on the ground. I was out cold."

I shuddered, "And have you ever been riding since?"

"Nope," he concluded with finality.

Now I understood his reluctance, his claim of complete inexperience, and what a good sport he was to try again.

The next morning we rose bright and early, reporting to the head wrangler, Carol Thorpe. She called the numerous guests one by one, assigning each to a horse her practiced eye told her would be an appropriate match. "Anne?" she said, checking her clipboard.

"Here!" I replied promptly.

"Experienced rider?"

"Yes," I said, with more confidence than I felt.

"You're on Buck," she said, pointing out a handsome buckskin gelding. "Ron?"

He stepped forward smartly. "Here!"

"You listed, 'Never been on a horse before'?"

"Well, only once, and that was very briefly. It wasn't a satisfying experience—for me *or* the horse!" he answered with a wry smile.

"Well, then," she chuckled, "we'll put you on Nehi. He's a horse we use for beginners and children."

Ron looked relieved. While the other guests were saddling up and having stirrups adjusted, he was reading something intently. I didn't know what it was at the time, but later discovered it was a reprint of an article that Carol's husband, Jim, had written for the local newspaper. It was titled "How to Ride a Horse."

One by one, the various groups of riders started out on the Lodge's extensive trail system. For over an hour we meandered through the stands of sweet-smelling piñon pines and junipers that covered the red rock foothills below the Santa Fe National Forest. Clumps of fragrant sagebrush, chamisa, and scrub oak accented the spectacular scenery. Black-chinned and broad-tailed hummingbirds whirred overhead in the startlingly blue sky. Small, squirrel-like animals chattered and scolded as we rode by their burrows.

We finally emerged onto a broad, flat mesa where we were met by the tantalizing smells of sizzling bacon, griddle cakes, and jalapeño seasoned fried potatoes with onions. That kind of stuff just about goes straight from your mouth to your coronary arteries without even passing through your stomach!

It tasted wonderful.

"Well, what do you think?" I asked Ron between mouthfuls.

"About the food or the ride?"

"Both."

"Great!" he replied with a broad grin. "I really enjoyed the food *and* the ride."

"How 'bout going again tomorrow?" I asked eagerly.

"Whoa! Let's see how we feel when we get up in the morning. I might be a little sore," he demurred.

He felt fine the next day so we went again, this time on a little longer ride. Despite his unfortunate early childhood experience, Ron had a natural riding ability that amazed both himself and the wranglers. He soon graduated to a more lively horse and was finally 'promoted' to Chief Joseph, a tall, gangly Appaloosa that quickly became his favorite mount. As Ron's confidence grew, we gradually extended the rides onto steeper, more challenging trails.

He loved it.

Every night after dinner we trekked out to the corral like a couple of kids, pockets stuffed with carrots and apples for the horses. Buck soon recognized our footsteps and headed toward the fence when he heard us coming, laying his ears back and warning the other horses off with a dismissive snort. Joe, shy and unaggressive, usually hung back until Ron coaxed him up with soft clucks and gentle words of encouragement.

When we returned to Salt Lake City, Ron eagerly recounted his horseback riding adventures to his brothers. He attributed much of his initial success to reading Jim Thorpe's helpful hints. "I never realized you're supposed to ride using your legs, not your seat!" he enthused.

Keith, the youngest, laughed. "Well, sure, Ron. You can learn to do a lot of things if you can read!"

The following January, Ron was sorting through the mail one evening as I fixed dinner. His face brightened. "Ha! We just got our reservations confirmed for next summer at the Bishop's Lodge," he announced.

"You're excited," I responded.

"I miss Joe," he confessed somewhat sheepishly. "I'm really looking forward to seeing him again."

"I'm not jealous," I teased. "It's okay to have an additional 'significant other'—as long as it's a horse!"

The next summer, Ron was eager to return to Santa Fe and could hardly wait for our first ride. When we approached the corral, Joe whickered at Ron in recognition. Ron, inordinately pleased, exclaimed, "He remembers me!"

Indeed he did.

As we saddled up and headed into the mountains, Ron and Joe hung back a bit. Joe was walking placidly, one ear flopped over in relaxation and eyes half closed in pleasure as Ron murmured to him quietly. Every line of Ron's body bespoke pure enjoyment.

Denusha, one of our favorite wranglers, looked back and chortled. "I don't know who's more contented," she commented, "the man or the horse!"

Near the end of our stay, Ron and I were both eager to venture beyond the well-worn Lodge trails. Denusha offered to take us on a long private ride to the aspen meadows high in the Sangre de Cristo mountains.

We packed lunches, water, and the sketchy hiking maps we had found in local mountaineering stores. A brief rainstorm during the night had freshened the sparkling air and dampened the dirt trails. The pines and junipers emitted pungent odors as we brushed by them on our way up the mountain.

Ron rode Joe, of course. I was on Buck, the handsome gelding; he was well into the equine equivalent of middle age but still loved to gallop until the wind made my eyes tear. Denusha was on Mercedes, a spirited, coal-black mare of indeterminate lineage and disproportionate conformation who nevertheless had the stamina of a well-conditioned triathlete.

The horses, eager and well rested, walked so fast we were at the aspen meadow before lunchtime. Denusha looked at her watch and grinned mischievously. "We've still got lots of time left," she announced. "Want to go exploring?"

"Sure!" we both exclaimed enthusiastically.

She gave Mercedes a squeeze with her legs and off they went, straight up the side of a steep hill, propelled like a rocket by the mare's powerful hindquarters.

We followed. Before long we were riding on unkempt, rarely used trails. Overhanging branches and dense undergrowth lined the narrow paths, scraping against us as the horses wove back and forth between the closely spaced trees.

We retraced our route several times, following the barely visible trail. Eventually the faint track petered out completely, ending blindly on a steep ridge that overlooked a box canyon.

Denusha paused, then pulled out the map. A bad sign.

"We're not lost, are we?" I asked anxiously.

"Naw," Ron put in with good humor. "We're not lost. We just don't know where we are!"

I didn't think that was very funny. When I didn't laugh, his smile faded. "Are we really lost, Denusha?" he questioned soberly.

"Yep," she replied. Strangely enough, she didn't seem worried. Not in the least.

"Why aren't you worried?" I demanded, somewhat annoyed at her casual attitude.

" 'Cause the horses aren't lost," she answered calmly. "*We* may be lost. But *they* always know which way home is. Especially good ol' Buck. He knows for sure."

I was astonished. "You mean all those old stories about lost or injured cowboys tying themselves into the saddle during a blizzard and the horse taking them all the way home are for real?"

"Sure," she replied matter-of-factly. "Watch. You lead. Just let Buck have his head."

"Okay," I said dubiously, nudging Buck to the front of our threesome. I would have bet he had never been on that overgrown trail so far from the Lodge's familiar territory.

Buck strode out confidently and steadily. Neck arched proudly, his ears swiveled forward in watchful alertness as he led our small group down the mountain.

You can guess the end of the story. Three hours and a brief lunch break later, we were back at the corral. Faithful Buck was rewarded with an extra ration of bran mash. We took a hot bath.

One of the most comforting, reassuring things I've learned as a convert to the Church is that the Brethren always know where "home" is. *Always.* Outsiders may think it naive and doubters may scoff, but I firmly believe you simply can't go wrong by following the First Presidency and the Twelve. They know the sure way, even when the trail seems faint or imperceptible to the rest of us.

In a recent conference address, Elder L. Aldin Porter reminded us: "He whom the Lord has called and we have sustained is not a novice in the principles, process, and practice of receiving divine direction.

"There is a question that each of us must deal with in a most solemn and serious way if our lives are to be what the Father of us all would have them be. 'What is our response when the living prophets declare the mind and the will of the Lord?'

"I sat in this tabernacle some years ago as President Joseph Fielding Smith stood at this pulpit. It was the general priesthood meeting of April 1972, the last general conference before President Smith passed away. He said, '*There is one thing which we should have exceedingly clear in our minds. Neither the President of the Church, nor the First Presidency, nor the united voice of the First Presidency and the Twelve will ever lead the Saints astray or send forth counsel to the world that is contrary to the mind and will of the Lord*'" (*Ensign*, November 1994, p. 63).

So if you'd trust a horse, why not God's prophet?

Chapter 19

And What About Anna?

The manuscript was nearly complete. As I read the final draft of *The Simeon Solution,* I reflected once more on that after-dinner discussion when our doctor friend and neighbor had first talked about the concept. What would he think?

On the spur of the moment, I picked up the telephone and called. "I hate to impose on your free time, but . . . " I said, briefly outlining what I had been doing with his idea.

"Come on over," he replied warmly, dismissing any hesitation I'd had about bothering him.

I felt strangely diffident as I walked the few blocks to his house. How would he react? Would he be pleased?

He had just returned from the office and was busy feeding the dog. We sat in the kitchen chatting amiably as his youngest daughter bounced in and out of the room for periodic assistance with her homework. I asked him if he remembered that evening long ago when he had told us about the Simeon Solution.

"Of course. I've thought a lot about that discussion," he answered. "I'm pleased it was helpful."

"*Very,*" I emphasized. "It put into words some of the concepts I'd been developing for a long time. How to trust the Lord. Stay

148

faithful. Remain focused and centered. Be patient. How to meet adversity with equanimity. That sort of thing."

He nodded. "You know, you and I were both undergraduates in the 'sixties. It was a time of unrest, of uncertainty. In some respects, it wasn't much different from what we face today."

"You're right," I agreed. "Except now the voices of dissent and negativism somehow seem louder, more shrill."

"Simeon also lived in turbulent times," he added. "Yet he believed. And he patiently trusted the Lord, waiting a lifetime to behold the promised Messiah."

"Maybe perspective is also enhanced with age. You know, being fifty instead of twenty or thirty helps!" I grinned.

"Perhaps," he agreed slowly. "But I think we can all learn to stay rooted. Centered. Grounded. To keep things in context and be able to put aside unanswered concerns and questions."

"Not always easy," I admitted.

He grew serious, reflecting. "When I was an undergraduate back East, one of the Brethren who was then an Assistant to the Twelve visited the student ward. We had a chance to chat privately. He made me feel comfortable in expressing my concerns. I had some doctrinal questions for which there seemed to be no answers."

He continued, "To my surprise, he replied, 'You know, I don't have all the answers either. But I take those questions and, figuratively speaking, put them on the shelf. I can do that because I know the Church is true.'

"I've never forgotten that wise counsel," he finished. "When I read about Simeon, it made sense. That's what I meant by being able to put your concerns and questions on a spiritual 'back burner.'"

Thanking him for his ideas and input, I started to leave.

He stopped me. "And what about Anna?" he asked.

149

"Anna?" I replied blankly.

"Yes, Anna. She was there too. She also recognized Jesus as the promised Messiah. Are you going to say anything about her?" he said, reaching for his scriptures.

Sure enough. There it was, also in the second chapter of Luke: "And there was one Anna, a prophetess, the daughter of Phanuel, of the tribe of Aser: she was of a great age, and had lived with an husband seven years from her virginity;

"And she was a widow of about fourscore and four years, which departed not from the temple, but served God with fastings and prayers night and day.

"And she coming in that instant gave thanks likewise unto the Lord, and spake of him to all them that looked for redemption in Jerusalem" (Luke 2:36–38).

"So what about Anna?" I said. "Faithful, righteous women throughout the ages have received personal revelation. In that sense, we can all be prophets or prophetesses. With a small 'p,'" I added.

"But what about with a large 'p'? As in Prophet and Priesthood?" he persisted. "What's your answer to that?"

"The same as it was several years ago when we had the dinner party: I don't know. And that's still okay. I don't have to have answers to all my questions. Thanks to you—and the Simeon Solution—I can live with that. In fact, I feel even a greater sense of peace now than I did then. I know the Church is true with all my heart. And that's sufficient," I concluded.

He smiled. "For me too. It really works."

Indeed it does. I return again and again to the simple principles of the Simeon Solution:

1. *Trust the Lord.*
2. *Learn to recognize and heed spiritual promptings.*
3. *Focus on the fundamentals.*
4. *Stand firm in the faith.*
5. *Be patient.*
6. *Adopt the eternal perspective.*
7. *Keep the commandments.*
8. *Know the Church is true.*

None of those basic concepts is independent of the others. They are all necessary. They interrelate and combine harmoniously to form a firm spiritual center, the "place of safety" that provides refuge and comfort in times of need.

The most precious blessings of my life have come directly through the gospel of Jesus Christ. The things that I know most surely are known not by intellect but by the Spirit. I know that if I live worthily, someday I too, like Simeon, will say: "Lord, now lettest thou thy servant depart in peace, according to thy word: For mine eyes have seen thy salvation" (Luke 2:29–30). The things I don't know, the questions I still have, can wait. I can be patient. I trust the Lord's promises.

And that is enough.